BRITISH RAILWAYS ILLUSTRATED
ANNUAL No. 4

IRWELL
PRESS

CONTENTS

LEAN & KEEN :
Converted Coppertops
E1 and D1 4-4-0s of the Southern
By R.H.N. Hardy 4

GRANTHAM
Hub of the Great Northern
By Eric Neve 28

NOCTURNE
.... 36

WAR REPORT
.... 38

DIESEL DAWN
V Signs of the Times
.... 46

LEICESTER'S MODERN
ROUNDHOUSE
By Ian Sixsmith 47

ON THE MILK
.... 62

Station Survey
ABERDEEN JOINT
By Keith G. Jones and
Oswald Patterson 84

SUBSCRIPTIONS

Readers can subscribe for six or twelve issues at a time to the magazine. The cost for six issues is £13.20 inclusive of postage and packing whilst twelve issues are charged at £26.40. Overseas subscribers should add the cost of surface/air mail. Limited numbers of back issues are also available - see separate notice. All remittances should be made out to IRWELL PRESS MAGAZINES LTD and sent to :-

The General Manager's Office,
P.O.Box 1260, Caernarfon,
Gwynedd, LL55 3ZD
Telephone :
General Manager:- 01286 871775
Office Enquiries:- 01286 871776
Fax : 01286 871605

Cover Photo: MINORU waiting to depart King's Cross, August 1952. G.F.Heiron.

Rear Cover: 45024 on LM goods.

Frontispiece:- GLASFRYN HALL leaving Temple Meads June 1955. G.F.Heiron.

Printed & Bound by Amadeus Press
Copyright :- Irwell Press 1995

Welcome to **British Railways Illustrated Annual No.4,** a Christmas treat now raised almost to institutional stature. You'll never be *mogadored* with a BRILL Annual, and for an explanation of that arcane term see **Richard Hardy's** account of Southern 4-4-0s in **Lean and Keen: Converted Coppertops.** These engines were seldom *mogadored* either and the following extract sums up Richard Hardy's enthusiasm for these diminutive jewels: *The Maunsell 'Rebuilds' were one of the all time greats amongst the small engines of this country, an amazing quart in a pint pot, a conversion of the Edwardian Wainwright D and E class into a virile fiery steed, capable of great things, with long travel valves, a big firebox and yet no disadvantages when it came to maintenance and repairs: the brainchild of thinking and experienced engineers who were not afraid to look at what was going on elsewhere, especially in Wiltshire some 77 miles from Paddington.* Richard Hardy discusses the development and the complex lineage of these engines, marrying a technical account to experiences at Stewarts Lane in the 'fifties and ending with the engines' swan song on the Faversham jobs and its 'Fan Club' of timing specialists, Norman and Arthur Harvey and Syd Nash.

It has been a momentous year for anniversaries; so many years have passed now that people can look back not only on VE Day and VJ Day but their commemoration too, half a century on. To the question *What Did You Do On VE Day?* there are doubtless many replies - some near-heroic, some absurd with a fair few, like its 1995 equivalent, involving suitable quantities of ale. Well, in **War Report** we have a man, **Sapper with a Camera,** who spent it in eminently sensible fashion - a man who celebrated VE Day by bunking his nearest shed, the GWR at Oswestry, secure in the knowledge that after six weary years, on this day of all days restrictions, at last, would not be enforced.

One of the reasons for our series of *Annuals* and *Summer Specials* was the problem of presentation - quite a few subjects demanded a more generous treatment than was possible in a magazine of 56 pages, in which the balance between the subjects, both historical and geographical, has to be observed. The various vanished traffics of BR are each a vast subject, concerned in turn with all the many facets - the buildings and yards, the business itself, the organisation, the services and the locos and vehicles. **On the Milk** is a stab at bringing back to life the once vast and intricate system of getting this everyday (once an almost vital necessity for parts of the populace) foodstuff onto our tables.

You'll find a lot about engine sheds in the pages of BRILL; they were after all the lair of the beast which so fascinated us all and, the British railway enthusiast being a law abiding sort, such establishments were the only places where most of us regularly and deliberately set out to commit an offence - the heinous crime of trespass. But was a trainspotter *ever* prosecuted? Your stories welcome. Sheds in Britain owed their development and design, their layout and the look of their architecture, to threads which can be traced, in often highly individual - even eccentric - fashion, all the way back to the 1870s. The final development of engine shed practice in Britain, its apogee if you like, came, unexpected and unsung, in the East Midlands of England, in the form of the **Leicester Roundhouse** - appropriately enough it was a Midland Railway site - belonging once to a company which had been at the forefront of shed building a hundred years before. It was a company best known of course, for its - roundhouses .

Station Survey is a classic feature of BRILL and appropriately enough, here in the *Annual* is contained a bumper version - the great Joint station at Aberdeen providing a fine backdrop for some splendid pictures of both LM and LNE power.

Almost at the other end of the East Coast was Grantham and an account of its locomotives and work, **Hub of the Great Northern** is the very last writing of the late Eric Neve and a fitting tribute, for the subject was his especial joy.

IRWELL GENUINE TRACK PLANS - BEWARE CHEAP IMITATIONS

You'll remember those black and white days

1549, the engine that tore through Faversham, safety vales roaring, when I saw her in 1954. She is in pre-war Southern livery at Lewes on a Brighton - Tonbridge train but remained almost unchanged to her day of reckoning in 1956. Photograph J. Tatchell Collection.

LEAN AND KEEN: Converted Coppertops
E1 and D1 4-4-0s of the Southern

By R.H.N. Hardy

On a Saturday afternoon in the high summer of 1954. Stewarts Lane shed was in its usual state of organised turmoil and, as Shedmaster, I felt that I could afford to go down the Chatham road on a Faversham 'River' (a U class Mogul) with Driver Alf Murray and a young fireman, not quite sure of himself. The grate on a 'River' did not slope a great deal so the fire had to be level to get the best results. So I went as far as Faversham and, as things were going well, left them to it and waited for an up train with Stewarts Lane men. Kent was full of trains that day. The first one up went through with an unrebuilt 'Coppertop' No.1549, class D, built in 1906, on nine coaches, blowing off hard and all set to rush the climb towards Teynham. Our men were in splendid form on a engine that had but two years to go before making its final journey. What other railway than the Southern would be using an Edwardian wet steam 4-4-0 on a nine coach express in 1954? Sole Street bank would tax the old lady but most of the Wainwright engines would steam

when they were thrashed and no time was lost that day by 1549.

So, for the next half an hour, I was treated to a lesson in 'Chatham' locomotive history which will serve as an introduction to this article. First a 'German', a class L 4-4-0. It may have been built in Manchester by Beyer Peacock or in Berlin by A. Borsig in 1914 but, to us, the whole class were 'Germans'

D class on a Charing Cross - Deal express via Dover. A740 has a fair load and is hard at work attacking the 1 in 120 through Chelsfield up to Knockholt, about 1930. The smokebox door has warmed up but the safety valves are sizzling so the enginemen will be happy. Photograph J. Tatchell Collection.

A Ramsgate L class 31764, passing Factory Junction on 23rd August 1958, on the last lap to Victoria, load nine coaches. To us she was a 'German' although built in 1914 by Beyer Peacock - she continued on Kent Coast work until displaced by electrification in 1959. Photograph R.C. Riley.

and good old sloggers they were, not flyers on the level but strong on the banks. They would have been superheated Wainwright engines, with piston valves, at the hand of Robert Surtees who had done a good job for the London Chatham and Dover at Longhedge before going to Ashford as Chief Draughtsman of the SECR under Wainwright, but when R.E.L.

Maunsell took over in 1914 as CME, he sent the L class drawings to his old Great Southern & Western Drawing Office at Inchicore whence he had come and some changes were recommended, including a reduction of the steam lap from one and a sixteenth inch to seven eighths of an inch, with consequently shortened valve travel. So the 'Germans' lost some of the free-

dom of movement on level roads enjoyed by the original slide valve 'Coppertops' but they were good engines for all that and this one belonged to Faversham.

A few minutes later came a 'Glasshouse' L1 on a stopping train from Dover. These were very fine engines, strong and fast and yet they were but a modification of the 'Germans', made

A true 'German', built by Borsig of Berlin in June 1914. 1772 at Tonbridge bound for Ashford and Margate via Canterbury West in 1948. A very graceful locomotive, she looks good in the malachite green, which was hard wearing and a pleasure to clean. Photograph J. Tatchell Collection.

A Dover L1, 31753, attached to a West Country and about to go on the pit at Stewarts Lane after assisting the up Night Ferry (probably via Chatham) in 1957. A good strong combination for this very heavy train and road. Photograph J. Tatchell Collection.

to satisfy an urgent traffic need in 1926 rather than a new creation. The L front end was retained but, by adjustment of the eccentrics and alteration of the rocking lever arms, the valve travel was increased as far as the length of the steam chest would allow, to give steam lap of one and three sixteenths inch and a travel of five and three eighths of an inch in full gear. The 'Germans' were never similarly altered which was a pity, but money was always tight. As it was, the L1s did brilliant work with 350 ton trains on the 80 minute Folkestone - Charing Cross flyers and made their name all over the railway. Our men liked them better than the L class but we had none at Stewarts Lane and the Germans had long gone to the country by 1952. I had a moderate journey on an L with Faversham men from Chatham to Sittingbourne and a very good one on a L1 with our Driver Syd Patrick from Faversham to Victoria. Having relieved the country men, he made himself comfortable on the fireman's seat and told me to get on with the driving, which was fine and dandy until we got to Chatham where the platform inspector came up to tell Syd that he was going to Victoria via the North Kent and did he know the road? Of course he did, for most of the Eastern men at Battersea and the Old Kent Road would have died rather than admit they didn't know their way around Kent. Much of the North Kent was new to me but Syd kept me at it all the way home via Strood, Dartford, Woolwich, Blackheath and Nunhead. That was my one trip on an L1 - comfortable, plenty of room in the cab and all the controls positive and to hand. A good machine with a deep and throaty bark, rather than a sharp exhaust.

Back to that high summer Saturday afternoon - in came a single chimney 'Schools' from Ramsgate, to stop at the platform with Ramsgate men and I

think it was 922, my old school 'Marlborough'. There is no need for me to say much about those remarkable machines. They were much bigger and very different to the four coupled engines already mentioned but they had their little ways. Whereas the D, E, L and L1 had a flat grate and needed firing thin and all round the firebox, the 'Schools' had a steeply sloping grate and it was absolutely essential to keep the fire built up above the level of the bottom of the firehole door when working hard, otherwise the backend would go down the slope, which was the quickest way to a 100lb of smoke and no steam. And, if by chance you think that I am stretching it, let me tell that, at the age of all but 70, it happened to me, not once but three times in a day with 926 on the North Yorkshire Moors Railway in 1993. I was old enough to

know better and I was far from pleased with myself.

Most of the Ramsgate men worked their 'Schools' on about 40% cut off and the first port of the regulator, often eased back to about 60psi in the steam chest, just like an old GC man driving an 'ROD'. If the 'Schools' had a fault, it was rough riding and such working was said to ease wear and tear in the coupled axleboxes and motion. One time I came up from Herne Bay with a Ramsgate man who ran the whole way on 40% cut off except for the climb from Cuxton Road up to Sole Street where he shortened his cut off to 30-35% and put the regulator into the big valve. As soon as we were over the top, back he went to 40%. What would the great Cecil J. Allen have made of that? So away went 922, quietly and confidently, and the stage was set for the arrival of the next up train.

Checked outside the station, it approached slowly with an exhaust worthy of a big Great Western engine but it was no giant, simply a little 52 ton 4-coupled 'Converted Coppertop', No.1504, a Stewarts Lane engine with our men and nine coaches. The Maunsell 'Rebuilds' were one of the all time greats amongst the small engines of this country, an amazing quart in a pint pot, a conversion of the Edwardian Wainwright D and E class into a virile fiery steed, capable of great things, with long travel valves, a big firebox and yet no disadvantages when it came to maintenance and repairs: the brainchild of thinking and experienced engineers who were not afraid to look at what was going on elsewhere, especially in Wiltshire some 77 miles from Paddington. But on this particular Saturday, the train stood in the back platform to allow a West Country with a very heavy boat train to pass and while this was happening, I took stock of 1504. We had 120psi, coal all over the footplate and two of the most

Ashford in 1948 and an L1 looking its best in malachite green. The snifting valve behind the chimney were sensibly removed by Bulleid and the prominent pipe from the smokebox carried steam to the exhaust injector. Photograph R.C. Riley.

A67, still with SECR plate on the cabside, passing Bickley en route to Dover via Chatham with a seven car Pullman train. No fuss or smoke on the 1 in 95 and the safety valves just buzzing. Photograph J. Tatchell Collection.

A67 again, renumbered 31067, passing Factory Junction with the 13.42 Dumpton Park - Victoria. One of the 1919 E1 rebuilds, she has put in 38 years of hard work since conversion. There will be about nine coaches, the sort of train that was easy money for all concerned with a 'Converted Coppertop'. The engine has lost its Wakefield mechanical lubricator, once regarded as a necessity. Photograph R.C. Riley.

talkative men at Stewarts Lane. The fireman was G.W. Morris, who emigrated to Australia, and the driver, a certain 'Gramophone' Edgeley.

Now Bert Edgeley was no fool, indeed he was a pretty shrewd customer who had, on one occasion, turned the tables on me in a way that neither of us would forget. But he had been vaccinated with a gramophone needle. However, we made a start from Faversham with about 140psi and, at my instigation, G.W. got busy, tidied things up and we were soon round to the blowing off point. Bert was relatively silent and we did well to Chatham and then

attached the 1 in 100 of Sole Street bank. Half way up, going well with that marvellous sharp bark of an exhaust, we were brought to a stand. Our fireman returned from the telephone to say that a boat train had been stopped at the next signal and could not get started so we were to draw forward carefully until we found him to give a push up to Sole Street. By and by, we cracked the guard's detonators and were called forward until we squeezed buffers.

At the head of twelve and two vans was the West Country that passed us at Faversham. When he was ready to

start, we exchanged crows on the whistle and, without a slip but with deafening exhaust, that little 52 ton machine got the double train on the move with the Pacific slipping and sliding at the head. Our engine never faltered and we accelerated up the long bank, dropping off under the protection of the Sole Street signals. It was an experience that I shall never forget. We had six of these engines at Stewarts Lane, their numbers being 1743 and 1749 (class D1) and 1019, 1067, 1504, 1506 (class E1). In winter some were used on the normal booked workings which included a tour of Kent after an early start or late finish at Holborn Viaduct. I seem to think that they were the heaviest engines allowed into what had been the City terminal of the LC&DR. In summertime, they worked most things except the boat trains for which they had been originally designed and before we look at the reasons for what was a remarkable rebuild achieved in a very short time, let us take stock of Albert Edgeley and how he got the better of me one evening when I was hoping for a quiet hour at the desk after the office staff had gone home.

I was deep in some paperwork after a long, hard summer day in 1953. Such peace as there could be at Stewarts Lane was shattered by a thunderous knock on the door which opened immediately to admit Bert. Without pausing he advanced to my desk and said 'Guv'nor, I've a complaint to make' and began a tirade about management inefficiency thumping the table for good measure. I listened for a while but, my blood superheating, I hopped out of the chair

D class 'Coppertop' in all its glory. Beautiful lines, beautiful livery: handsome is as handsome does which is as well when one looks at the coal. The LBSC and LSW used good Welsh but not the Chatham! So the dart is handy on the tender to get the fire blazing hot for the heavy work ahead. Photograph J. Tatchell Collection.

The nearside of a D. Neither 493 nor 488 were rebuilt to D1 and lasted to 1954 and 1956 respectively. The classic Edwardian express passenger engine, simple, fast, strong, easy to maintain and clean; exactly what the Running people needed. Photograph J. Tatchell Collection.

and told him if he thought he could do my job, to come round and get on with it. I had read my Hamilton Ellis, who once wrote that Dugald Drummond was in the habit of terrorising men who dared to criticise his engines, by this method, but I was no Drummond and it was 1953, not 1900. So Bert nipped round the table and sat down in my chair while I banged some papers down in front of him as unpleasantly as possible. 'Try your hand at that bloody lot, you won't be so clever in future'. He looked at the top of the file for a minute and came up with the correct answer! We both burst out laughing, he forgot about his complaint and I don't doubt that he told the story a thousand times. As for me, it was yet another lesson in the fascinating and never ending study of human nature. Never underestimate anybody.

And now these 'Converted Coppertops'. The D class had had a copper capped chimney, not to mention a brass dome and the glory of the full Wainwright livery whilst the Es, with their slightly larger dimensions, Belpaire fireboxes and extended smokeboxes were even more impressively beautiful. They were straightforward and easy to maintain in every way, free steaming and fire throwing, free running and easy riding, lovely little engines within their limits. However, the 'Rebuilds' were neither elegant nor graceful but, even when stationary, they carried a remarkable aura of suppressed energy and dash which was immensely attractive to the eye. Some sort of a comparison can be drawn in general appearance with the slightly

heavier Midland class 2 4-4-0s - stately old things with a fair turn of speed but none too brisk in the uptake.

In 1919, the SECR management decided to develop wholeheartedly the Continental services via Dover and Folkestone and to concentrate them on Victoria, the West End terminal of the LC&DR. This railway had, of course, competed with the SER for boat train traffic before the 1899 amalgamation, after which much of its Dover work had been transferred to Charing Cross but the steam services from the suburbs

into Cannon Street and Charing Cross were growing fast. With an eye to ultimate electrification, the then General Manager took the wise decision to run the boat train services from Victoria, not only over the old SER routes via Tonbridge or Maidstone East but also on the LC&DR routes via Chatham. But one major difficulty had to be overcome, and very quickly at that...

The boat trains were to be both fast and heavy and to avoid double heading, it was necessary to use more powerful locomotives than the Ds and Es

516, the first E to be built, in 1908, with an extended smokebox, it was shown at the Franco-British exhibition the same year. The beautiful paintwork survived four years of constant cleaning and polishing. Passing Elmstead Woods, 516 is in good form with a heavy train, probably the 14.15 Charing Cross to Folkestone Junction. Photograph J. Tatchell Collection.

The same engine, the last to be painted grey in 1923, is passing Factory Junction and Wandsworth Road with an eight coach Dover boat train via Tonbridge. 516 is steaming freely, no fears for the long drag to Knockholt. On the left are the AC overhead structures of the LBSC South London line and, in the distance, Battersea Loco. and Hampton's Depository. Photograph J. Tatchell Collection.

which were the heaviest allowed over many of the LCDR bridges, especially at the London end. The Civil Engineer had already scheduled a comprehensive programme of bridge strengthening and track renewals to allow for heavier engines but the most urgent task was to complete the length be-

tween Victoria, Bickley and the Chislehurst loops, to give priority to boat trains going via Sevenoaks and Tonbridge. This would take some five years, after which work would be concentrated on Chislehurst - Dover via Faversham and Swanley to Ashford, via Maidstone. As both the 'Germans'

and the two Es, 36 and 275, which had been superheated and rebuilt with piston valves in 1912, were too heavy, there were no locomotives capable of handling 300 tons on the schedules of the day on a regular basis. The only alternative was to double head every train over 250 tons with class D, E, B1

Before the E1s arrived, the heavy Victoria boat trains were double headed, often with an F1 or B1 assisting a 'Coppertop'. The Stirling F and B had big cylinders and small domeless boilers but the Wainwright boiler transformed them and they became splendid rough old 'Flying Bedsteads' that would run, steam and stand a merciless thrashing. Climbing to Sydenham Hill, 140 is off down to Maidstone East and the PW man would never get his Track Safety Certificate today! Photograph J. Tatchell Collection.

or F1 in tandem, a situation which could not be tolerated for any length of time. Maunsell, who had already begun the modernisation of the SECR motive power with the introduction of his N and K class, incorporating several Swindon features to their great advantage, had to move quickly to create a locomotive capable of hauling 300 tons over all the heavy routes to Dover and Folkestone and yet weighing no more than the saturated D and E.

Maunsell was a sound engineer but he was also an outstanding manager who believed in delegation once he had created a team of far sighted and capable engineers. Additionally, he expected these engineers to move in high railway and engineering circles and to practise the art of 'Watching the World' for developments elsewhere. When he arrived from Inchicore in 1914, Wainwright's Chief Draughtsman, Robert Surtees, was about to retire and so Maunsell took the opportunity to bring in new blood from Swindon and also from the Midland, in the shape of James Clayton who became Chief Locomotive Draughtsman on Surtees' retirement. But Clayton, who had served his time with Beyer, Peacock and had wide experience before going to Derby, became Maunsell's right hand man, and in time his Personal Engineering Assistant. He had also brought in G.H. Pearson from Swindon as Works Manager and Assistant CME, a wise move as his views on Swindon design and practice prevailed

when Clayton's first plan was said to have been too conservatively Midland.

However, in 1917, with the end of the War in sight, a body called the Association of Railway Locomotive Engineers was set up to undertake, amongst other things, the design of suitable standard locomotives acceptable to any railway under the Grouping that was then envisaged and which actually came about in 1923. The ARLE duly met and decided on a 2-6-0 mixed traffic locomotive as a priority. Maunsell of the SECR undertook the work, which devolved upon Clayton and his staff. Clayton was often called into consultation by the senior engineers and was greatly impressed by Churchward (GWR) with his logical and practical approach to the problems under review. Although he retained a cautious Midland streak, which had to be overcome by those close to him who were more radical in approach, the 'Converted Coppertop' was the brainchild of James Clayton, who had learned so much of Swindon practice during his short time at Ashford.

The drawings for the conversion were submitted and passed by the Civil Engineer in November 1917 but it was not until a year later that 179, a class E, was taken into Ashford Works for rebuilding. The weights on the coupled wheels of the wet steam E were 17ton 12cwt and 17tons 6cwt whereas the comparable weights on the L were 19tons 5cwt and 18tons 9cwt. The totals were 52 tons 5cwts and 57tons

9cwt but the weights of the superheated, modernised E1 were 17ton 5cwt and 16ton 0cwt with a total weight of 52ton 5cwt, the same as the wet steam E! So how was it done? In the first place, 179 was truly a rebuild as the frames, coupled wheels, bogie, boiler barrel and much of the motion was used. Secondly, the design was a blend of the N class 'Mogul' which incorporated Swindon practice and the existing E and so few, if any, parts were needed at the sheds that were not interchangeable. However, far greater power had to be generated to work the heavy boat trains and so the basis of the design was to enlarge the grate to burn more coal, to maintain a high degree of superheat and to replace the original slide valves by large diameter piston valves having ample port openings and longer laps. New cylinders of the same dimensions, 19ins x 26ins, with a saddle to carry a cylindrical smokebox, had 10ins piston valves above them and N class pistons and the smokebox, superheater, cab and boiler mountings were all modelled on the N. The eccentrics of the Stephenson valve gear were reset and rocking levers introduced to lengthen the valve travel, the piston valve heads were brought quarter of an inch closer than in the N, so increasing the steam lap to one and five eighths of an inch and giving an eighth inch exhaust clearance; the valve travel in full gear was six and a half inches. The chassis was stripped of all superfluous weight, the

After the Grouping, the F1s and B1s replaced the LBSC B2X and Gladstones on secondary work and also handled some of the commuter services from London Bridge and Victoria. B1 1101, of New Cross Gate, has brought some Pullman empties up to Victoria in 1938 before working to Oxted and Tunbridge Wells via Hever. Photograph J. Tatchell Collection.

B class No.13, having a tough old time climbing to Tattenham Corner with a Derby Week train of elderly six wheeled coaches. No telltale wisp of steam from those monstrous safety valves, the injector wasting water and the firehole door shut. The driver will be leaning on the wide open pull-out regulator handle, looking anxiously at pressure gauge and water level and hoping for the best; maybe they just made it without stopping for a 'blow up'! Photograph J. Tatchell Collection.

coupled wheel splashers reduced to a minimum width and the heavy tool boxes in the cab removed, whilst the cast iron drag box was replaced by one of fabricated steel. These were the essentials of the design, carried through with the great attention to detail that was to characterise Clayton's work in the years ahead. Certainly he had had experience of rebuilding class 2 locomotives at Derby, but on very conventional lines which bore no comparison

to what he was about to achieve at Ashford. It was natural, however, that he should call on his Derby experience, and this is revealed not only by the cut away running plate and the shape of the cab but in several other constructional details. There was perhaps a likeness in appearance to the Midland 2P but oh, the difference...

Thus Clayton achieved a remarkable modern rebuild, of the same weight as the E, though with far greater poten-

tial, but what was to be the effect of all this on the performance of 179? The boiler was already fitted with the Belpaire firebox but the flat grate was lengthened by increasing the slope to obtain 24 square feet. This large grate, along with relatively short flue tubes, made the boiler very free in steaming and at the same time, the superheater was capable of raising steam temperature to 650 - 700 degrees Fahrenheit, providing really hot steam that could

N 2-6-0 No.31811 was built in 1920, although 810 had entered service in August 1917 - many parts were interchangeable with the E1 The N was a very useful mixed traffic engine; unusually, the Walshaerts gear was arranged so that the dieblock was at the top of the link in fore gear, a feature also characteristic of the Us and Ks, as well as the Metropolitan Ks (a tank version of the N) and the Met. H 4-4-4 tanks, which had several Maunsell features. Photograph R.C. Riley.

179, class E, a beautiful Edwardian engine cleaned to the highest standards of 1910. The larger boiler, Belpaire firebox and extended smokebox add character, a certain raciness with enough copper and brass to keep the cleaners going all night. She will soon be on her way up the Chatham with a boat train for London. Photograph J. Tatchell Collection.

And here is the same engine, no brass or copper, grey paint and white numbers, the first 52 ton 'Converted Coppertop', but what a sight and sound as she climbs to Sydenham Hill at 1 in 100 with over 300 tons behind the tender! There is the fierce aggression, the blatant power, dash and enthusiasm of the modern locomotive. The safety valves have lifted, the stoker has just 'hit the right places' and all is well with the world. History is in the making. Photograph J. Tatchell Collection.

be used by the very efficient front end to generate power, out of all proportion to the size of the engine. At the same time great care had to be taken by both driver and fireman not to work the engine beyond the capacity of the boiler, for at 25% cut off, the port opening to steam was 0.5in. (against 0.33in. of a GW two cylinder 4-6-0) and with such a large opening the cylinders literally took their steam in 'gulps'. And how thrilling it was for me to learn by experience and over thirty years later, something of the challenge that had

been presented to the Battersea enginemen in the early days.

At the outset there was considerable difficulty with the lubrication of the cylinders and valve chests under such high superheat and, although 179 had been turned out in early February 1919, it was not until May, after the engine had taken over boat train work at Battersea, that the trouble was finally overcome by fitting large diameter oil pipes and a new type of four feed Wakefield mechanical lubricator. It was the enginemen who had most to

gain with so powerful an engine but there were still lessons to be learned pretty quickly. Apart from the new N class engines which were not used much by Battersea and Dover men at that time, the SECR engines had flat grates. The F1, both classes of 'Coppertop' and the 'Germans' had to be fired, little and often, round the box to maintain a thin, level fire. Do that, give them a good thrashing and they would steam for as long as the fireman could keep abreast of the water level in the boiler, but the 'Converted Coppertop' needed a different technique.

With a steeply sloping grate, the blast on the fire when working heavily, together with the movement of the engine at speed, could draw the fire from under the firehole door up to the tubeplate with immediate effect on the steaming, as the fire at the front had to be dancing on the firebars to get the best results. There were many classes of engine elsewhere that could be similarly affected - for example, the GC 'Directors' and the 4 cylinder engines about to be turned out from Gorton and certain precautions had to be taken. With the N class and 179 it was found that the fire had to be maintained well above the level of the bottom of the firehole - indeed some firemen filled the firehole completely and when they knew that more coal was required at the sides of the firebox they would push the top of the crust forward and fire two or three shovelful to each side and then black the hol

160, class E1, running quietly into Dover Marine with the *Lord Warden Hotel,* its garage, a nice line in open tourers and a good suit of plusfours in the background. The fire will be thin and level and the big ends and rockers will have the muted knock of a well maintained engine coasting in full gear. Photograph Geoffrey Carr.

But this one of A67 tells a story. Shakespeare Tunnel, nearly at the Marine, under the cliff and watch your head! But there are signs of a rough trip. The valves are lifting when they should be quiet, the blower is just off the face to avoid blowing off, the bottom of the smokebox door is pretty warm and I'll wager the fire is heavy and has gone down the slope. Photograph J. Tatchell Collection.

out again! This method worked very well on the E1s but if one allowed the fire to get too thin at the back there would be trouble. I nearly said that this could be a recipe for disaster or at least a rough trip but the E1s could do amazing work when steam pressure was back to 130-140psi, instead of the 180 to which the boiler was pressed.

So 179 made her mark and the SECR never looked back. Such was Maunsell's confidence in his (then un-tried) rebuild that, on February 12th 1919, five days after 179 had left the Ashford Erecting Shop, he sought authority - immediately granted - to re-build twenty more E1s. In the event, the only manufacturer that was able to undertake the work was Beyer Peacock and then only to the tune of ten engines but the last of the ten was in traffic by September 1920. In all major details, they followed 179 but they were slightly heavier, with 17.5 tons on the leading coupled axle, improved lubrication for the valves and pistons and slightly enlarged superheaters. In October 1919, Beyer Peacock offered to accept ten more E class for rebuilding during 1921 and the first of these were to go to Gorton in November 1920. Now the Es were slightly stronger and newer engines than the original D class and during 1920 G.H. Pearson, as Assistant CME (who had worked with Clayton on the design of 179 and who was a Swindon man) informed Maunsell that the E1 boiler and cylinders could be fitted to the D class without the expense of new or length-ned frames. Beyer Peacock agreed to

the change without extra charge and the last of the ten D1s was in service by November 1921. The two classes were almost identical, though the D1 had larger coupled wheels, 6ft 8ins against 6ft 6ins of the E1. The coupled wheelbase of the D1 was 6ins shorter and the engine weighed slightly less at 51tons 5cwt. Whereas the E1 had the same top feed as the N class, the D1 had clackboxes on the boilerside and sight feed lubrication instead of the mechanical lubricator of the E1. If

anybody wanted to determine which was which, he looked at the side rods which were plain on the D1 and fluted on the E1. To us, thirty years later, they were all 'Converted Coppertops' and there was nothing to chose between the two classes, for both were equally brilliant.

When new, the E1s went to Battersea, Dover and Margate not only for the boat trains but also the hardest Kent Coast services, such as the up and down Granville expresses.

A179 was painted Southern green, which suited her well, in March 1924. The original boiler has been changed for one carrying Ramsbottom safety valves but the top feed is in evidence and, of course, Stirling steam reversing gear. Photograph J. Tatchell Collection.

Factory Junction again, with A179 in good form, in 1924. There are six red Pullmans in a train of eight coaches bound for Dover via Tonbridge. The third rail is already laid on the fast lines and the up relief is being relayed. One could drop down to Battersea shed or go left for the West London or Clapham Junction. Photograph J. Tatchell Collection.

When the D1s came out, the allocation was strengthened at all three sheds whilst two were sent to Bricklayers Arms. By 1925, the N15 'Scotch Arthurs' took over the principal boat train work but they were too heavy for the Kent Coast from Faversham to Ramsgate, so the 'Rebuilds' continued to bear the brunt of the ever increasing traffic with great enthusiasm until 1932, when the 'Arthurs' were at last allowed beyond Faversham.

Now, there was another engineer whose name I have not mentioned but who played a considerable role in the development and improvement of the E1s and D1s. I was honoured to meet him briefly on two occasions and to listen to him on the subject of the remarkable rebuilds in the design of which, to his lasting regret, he played no part. This was Harold Holcroft, who served his time at Wolverhampton, Stafford Road and who had joined

Maunsell at Ashford in 1914 from Swindon where he had been involved in some of the great locomotive design work for which G.J. Churchward had been responsible, work which had reached its peak by 1910. Maunsell appointed him to undertake the preparation of plans for the extension and reorganisation of Ashford Works to which enterprise the declaration of War put paid. He was then loaned to the Railway Executive Committee and did not return to locomotive work until the last months of 1918, when 179 was well on the way to completion. He was then directed to work up the design of the three cylinder development of the N class 2-6-0 No.822, which ultimately appeared with the Holcroft derived motion for the middle engine.

When Maunsell took over from H.S. Wainwright, Locomotive Running was rightly set up as a separate department so that he could be designated Chief Mechanical Engineer whilst A.D. Jones, still well remembered by our Battersea enginemen in the early 'fifties, was appointed Locomotive Running Superintendent, reporting to the General Manager. However, Maunsell wanted a direct source of information on the performance of his locomotives through one of his senior engineers who was expected to work closely with the Running people regarding the organisation of various tests and trials. Holcroft had the good fortune to be chosen by Maunsell to travel on footplates as an observer for three years from January 1921 until design work of even greater importance claimed his attention after the Grouping and the transfer of the Ashford staff to Water-

Here is the direct comparison between E1 and D1 - see next page - at Battersea in 1922. On 160, the E1, we can see the mechanical lubricator and its drive from the leading coupled wheel, top feed and possibly the Anderson bypass between the bogie wheels. Never referred to in print, the device had been removed from both classes by the end of the 'twenties. The Battersea painter is at work for 160 was being prepared for the State visit of the King and Queen of Belgium in May 1922. Photograph Lens of Sutton.

D1 489, converted in July 1921 by Beyer Peacock. 6ft 8in coupled wheels, 9ft coupled wheelbase against the 9ft 6in of the E1 with 6ft 6in wheels, both reflecting the original dimensions. The boiler clack valves are on the side of the barrel and the front end is fed by sight feed lubrication as were our four Stewarts Lane E1s by 1952. The side rods are plain and those on 160 are fluted as on the original engines. At Stewarts Lane we never gave a thought to such detail - just got on with the job of running the railway. Photograph Lens of Sutton.

loo. It was the sort of task that the late D.W. Harvey would have loved and Holcroft's temperament enabled him to be immediately accepted by Running men in all grades whose outlook on life was, by necessity, very different from those responsible for design. Holcroft got things done for the Running people and during those three years he made some 170 trips on the E1s alone, all of which he got to know on a 'personal' basis. Posterity is fortunate indeed that he recorded these activities

in the second part of *Locomotive Adventure,* a most interesting and revealing work.

It is fascinating to read, amongst the many trials undertaken, of his involvement in getting the E1 No.506 to steam, the 'Black Sheep' of the 'Converted Coppertops' at Battersea. Holcroft made 47 trips with this engine whilst alterations were made to the draughting, the smokebox diaphragm plates and to the brick arch, as well as a thorough valves and pis-

tons overhaul in Ashford Works. Far greater than with any other member of the class was the frequency with which the fire went down the slope to the front end of the grate, even when the engine was being worked quite easily. For example, on 23rd May 1923 the engine had gone back to Battersea after some trials from Ashford and had been set to work on the boat trains without much improvement. Holcroft rode with Driver Woods and Fireman Gingell - yes, it was the immortal Sam in his younger days. He must have been in the Spare Link at the time because he did not start at Battersea until he was 21 in 1913. Aged 77, old Sam, who had only had one day off sick in his working life, undertook a drastic cure for shingles by spending a weekend on the SNCF and, on his return to Calais, firing with great success, the PLM Pacific 231G42 on the 'Fleche d'Or' from Amiens to Abbeville, where he was promoted to *Mecanicien de Route* by his French friends. However, back in 1923, he did not find his E1 No.506 so easy. He and Woods made a good start from Dover with an up Ostend boat train and passed Sandling with flying colours but then the fire slipped down the grate and performance began to deteriorate. By Tonbridge, the boiler pressure had fallen to 140psi with a loss of 1in in water level while by Knockholt it was back to 110psi with the water 4in down. Sam had been forced to mortgage the water level to keep going. Time

D1 in 1959, showing the Stirling steam reverser and gear, the piston valve cover and, n the cab, the damper control, sight feed lubricator and the double ended regulator andle. Sammy Gingell took Driver Bill Hoole of Kings Cross to Faversham on 1749. hey were a potent combination. Photograph R.C. Riley.

31506 starting from Bromley with 10 bogies up 1 in 95. Young Johnny Taylor is operating the reverser steam valve, the fireman is relaxed as the Ramsbottom valves lift, the sands are working and the blows must be put down to old age, for it is four months before the engine's last journey. But there will be some good stack music! Photograph R.C. Riley.

was more than kept to Tonbridge but a little was lost to Knockholt and the rest of the run was ruined by signal checks. But Sam will reappear before long, for he played a great part, along with many others, in the Indian Summer of those amazing engines.

By the 12th July 1923, the changes in the draughting on 506 had been finalised, an experimental larger chimney removed and the 5in blast pipe orifice reinstated. An experimental gap between the brick arch and the tube plate had been closed and the diaphragm plate extended in the smokebox. A trial from Ashford to Redhill and back showed that all was well and 506 was returned to Battersea. Here it did brilliantly and

Holcroft made his final observations on the 9th August on the 11.00 boat train from Victoria to Dover. The load was 289 tons and the average cut off 23% for most of the journey, with the regulator in the main valve for the uphill work. Despite some indifferent coal, the steaming was rock steady and the same could be said of 497, which had been similarly modified after giving some trouble. As a result of these practical but scientifically based trials, conducted by an able engineer with the dedicated support of the Running Department at all levels, the whole class and the D1s were still further improved and, to the best of my knowledge, no alterations of any consequence were made to the end of their days.

The last 'Converted Coppertop' was withdrawn from service in November 1961. It was the D1 No.739 which had by that time become 31739 and it had covered 2,002,974 miles since it was built in 1902. The last E1, No.31067, went earlier the same month but with lower mileage, having been built in 1908. The precursor of the class, 179, lasted until 1950 by which time it had covered 1,600,542 miles. It must be remembered in assessing these mileages, that the Southern operation was seasonal and passenger engines were often put into store for some of the winter months. When summer came, however, they more than earned their corn. Of the few minor changes, photographs tell us that what appeared to be Anderson cylinder by-pass valves were removed in the earlier Southern days. These must have been introduced by Clayton and would have been of little value either coasting or steaming on an engine with such freedom of movement. A photograph of 1507, taken in 1951, shows that the mechanical lubricator had been removed from the left hand framing, presumably to be replaced by the sight feed type: the top feed was gradually removed from the E1 boilers but not until 1948 was this finally achieved. Meanwhile, some D1s had appeared with top feed according to the allocation of the otherwise identical boiler at General Repair. By the early 'thirties, cylinder wear on some of the engines had developed to the extent that new cylinders of the same pattern and size had to be fitted whilst the frames of the D1s tended to fracture around and over the trailing coupled horns

E class A175, going hell for leather up the 1 in 120 by Chelsfield en route for London Bridge - Tunbridge Wells. The fireman has slipped a quick four or six round the level grate, the Ramsbottoms show their appreciation and the B Arms driver will certainly give her the works up the 1 in 53 out of Tonbridge. Photograph J. Tatchell Collection.

The first Borsig L class 1771, in service by June 1914, two months before 760 from Beyer Peacock, leaving Chislehurst tunnel with a 'Birdcage' set for Tunbridge Wells. Photograph J. Tatchell Collection.

Neither fault was prevalent in my time at Stewarts Lane - indeed, I cannot recall any serious mechanical derangement between 1952 and the end of 1954. And our six engines worked hard.

Back to the Present

So now let us walk down the yard towards the gloom of Stewarts Lane shed early in August 1952. For the first and last time, I came in over the iron bridge, near the Dewdrop, used by the spotters as they tried to edge by the Foreman's office at the outlet without detection. It was my first visit, I was to take up my duties a week later and from what I saw, I was not too sure what I should make of it all! I had never seen such smoke, nor heaps of ashes inside the shed, nor Bulleid Pacifics blowing off ramping mad, nor coal lying everywhere. Amid this bedlam, I asked the way to the office of the DMPS of a short, bow legged, bicycle clipped driver in his early 'fifties. He had just stabled a small passenger engine, bearing the number 31019, in front of the shed and was making his way to the Running Foreman's office - Driver Alf Murray, Battersea through and through, 1917 seniority, bombed out in the War and who died in Epsom Hospital in December 1994, aged 91, one of the very best in every way. On my way to the offices, I glanced at that

1781, the last Borsig to be delivered on the eve of the War. Enginemen spoke of their strength on the banks but said they were low on the level. But look at page 385 of the November 1924 *Railway Magazine* and you will find that 775 averaged 67.5 mph over the 25.6 miles from Smeeth to Paddock Wood with 285 tons. Not bad for an old German! Photograph R.C. Riley.

Alf Murray had berthed 31019 in front of Stewarts Lane shed as I walked in for the first time and here he is, eighty years of age, a railman at Ashtead and a well known character who retired a second time in 1982. A splendid mate who always encouraged the young; a keen ASLEF man, he was a credit to his calling. Photograph RHNH.

fierce little engine and felt that I was in the presence of something remarkable. I had not long to wait before I knew it for sure.

You must realise that, as an LNER man, I was not well acquainted with the Southern engines. It is true that I had read the two Brighton books by Burtt and J.N. Maskelyne, cover to cover, at an early age and that the works of a certain Dugald Drummond

were not unknown to me, but of the Chatham engines, my knowledge was limited to what I had learned from Mr. Cecil J. Allen in *The Railway Magazine* since I first read it at the age of six in January 1929. I was soon to learn that the SECR engines were superior to their counterparts on the Brighton and South Western although the superheated Drummond T9 was a very fine engine, greatly respected by the Chatham men, almost fit to be compared with that little 1019, standing on the front of the shed. Nor will you mind, I am sure, if I drop the 30000, for the only engines that carried this figure, in our book, were the Bulleid Pacifics and the 'Charlies', which had never been anything that could be comprehended. Everything else was referred to by its post-1931 Southern number, which saved time and trouble.

Why was 1019 'a fierce little engine?' The so-called Midland chimney with a capuchon at the front; the way it stood, seemingly leaning forward and eager to go; the cheeky little Ramsbottom safety valves buzzing gently; the strange and rather ugly dome cover, with a flat top, in two sections to facilitate removal, and then when one saw it moving in full gear, I marvelled at the immense travel of the rocking arms to which were attached valve spindles of a diameter I had never seen on any of 'our' engines. It was a tough little machine that would stand its ground and take on all comers, no frills, no nonsense, compact and efficient, a real fighter. 1019 stood quietly outside the shed but on my first Saturday I heard for the first time that remarkable bark which was the Rebuilds' very own. This time it was 1067 with ten coaches

bound for Ramsgate, every exhaust chopping off as sharp as could be, with the same driver, Alf Murray, whistling to us that all was well in their private world on a class of engine that had the touch of genius. This made them fascinating to control, sometimes wayward but always exciting and powerful as they tore into their work. The T9 had a more subtle and gentle ability, the steel hand in the velvet glove perhaps but with the Rebuild it was a frontal attack from the word go!

We were fortunate to have some of the remains of the old LCDR Longhedge Works in which work could be done at leisure in the winter months on the smaller engines, such as our six Rebuilds, the C, H and the E2s, the latter being our only Brighton engines. Here the work was carried out under very different conditions to the Running Shed, indeed, Longhedge was subject to Factory Act inspection which most certainly was not the case with the shed. Looking down the shop to the left, one saw a variety of machines as well as the forges and the small bays where the blacksmith, sheet metal worker, coppersmith and the whitemetaller worked their magic. The traverser, a rarity in locomotive depots in my experience, held the centre of the scene and to the right, one could see three, maybe four, small engines in various stages of repair. Detached from their tenders, they were shunted via the traverser into one of the side bays and every winter in their turn, the four E1s and two D1s were fettled up for the battle to come. Vic Smith, the chargehand, cheerful and talkative, Bert Snowball, an elderly fitter of great experience and one or two others, covered this vital work, often

No.19 spent much of her life at Battersea and Stewarts Lane. Early days - leaving Broadstairs, superheating well with a clean chimney top and a light load of seven SEC coaches and a Pullman. Photograph J. Tatchell Collection.

at Faversham and was made up of eight Maunsell corridor coaches, about 280 tons all told. The return working left Dover Priory at 14.02 and Faversham at 15.09. The 11.50 was part of Duty 18 and the return working, also with a Stewarts Lane engine, was 21. I cannot remember the other parts of these complicated two day duties but, almost certainly, there would have been a Holborn Viaduct involvement which merited the use of so light an engine. I joined our men at Victoria when they came onto the train; Driver 'Buster' Whiting and Fireman Harry Usher who, later on, fell out with his driver and left the railway. In fact, old Buster was one of the best but liked things his way, maybe a bit explosive but none the worse for that. Sadly, within eighteen months, he had died of cancer.

1019, as I first saw her at Stewarts Lane in August 1952. Working a special from Paddington to Robertsbridge in 1958, she stands on the centre road at Kensington as she must have done a thousand times on through trains from points north, east and west. Photograph R.C. Riley.

overseen by Bert Wood, our quietly humorous and capable Foreman Fitter, who did his paperwork most afternoons in the calm of the raised Victorian office which commanded a view of the whole shop. One felt that one had stepped back into history for it was forty eight years since the last Longhedge engine, 481, a C class goods, had been built in that very shop and yet here we were, in 1952, in the presence of the same old engines. Not

only that but we still had a genuine LCDR Kirtley engine, 201 built in 1891 which later became 1660, a class R 'Bobtail Tank' from which Surtees derived the well known H class, of which our old 1263 still does her stuff on the Bluebell Railway.

My first journey on a 'Converted Coppertop' was in October 1952. The engine was 1067 and the train was the then relatively unknown 11.50 SO Victoria - Ramsgate and Dover which split

The 11.50 was worked by No.2 Link which covered much of the Ramsgate work and, in winter, various bits and pieces such as the Gravesend - Farningham pull and push and much of the E1 and D1 work. I was struck by the simplicity of the cab layout of 1067 and the amount of room for such a small engine. The injector steam valves were operated by levers above the firebox, thus disposing with two fittings on the firebox backplate. There were no toolboxes or splashers in the cab, simply the damper control on the fireman's side nor was there a reversing rack in the driver's corner. When Surtees worked out the design of the C, D and H classes, he based each on his sound LCDR practices but on vir-

The 'Coppertops' F1 an B1 were all candidates for the Longhedge shop during the winter back in the 'thirties, and indeed later. 1728, D class, in Southern livery at Stewarts Lane, on the coal road after the modernisation in 1935. The pits are clear of ashes, as they were in my time at the Lane, for a detested a dirty shed and yard. Photograph Lens of Sutton.

tually all his engines he used the Stirling steam reverser, the best of its type that I ever encountered. It was positive, easy to maintain, quick but not too quick in action and strong enough to reverse a slide valve engine with some steam left in the steam chests, without having to wait all day, as with the Drummond reverser.

We were given a good push out of Victoria and so tore into the Grosvenor Road bank of 1 in 64. 'Buster' had notched up to 35% after a few revolutions and this with full regulator took us up onto the bridge without further adjustment, our exhaust ringing out sharp and clear, the sort of noise that makes the spine tingle. 25% and full regulator took us, when it was required, round the Catford loop, up to Bickley and on to the Swanley stop. In later years, this stop was deleted so that Farningham Road, at the foot of the bank from Swanley, could be rushed, to offset Longfield bank and the climb up to Sole Street. 'Buster' had used the first port of the regulator whenever the gradients would allow it and coasted at about 25% which seemed to suit the engine very well. It was very free running as was 1506 on the return from Faversham and, having watched the fireman on the outward run, I tried my hand from Faversham to Swanley. 1506 was using Blidworth coal from Stewarts Lane and Chislet from Dover, Notts hard and Kent soft, and I cannot recall having any difficulty on Sole Street bank or anywhere else. I kept filling the

firedoor, the standard practice with the E1 and D1, with the occasional shovelful to the sides and front of the firebox. It had been a happy start.

But to let that back end go was to court trouble. I learned a lesson very quickly on 1504, with Sammy Gingell and Les Penfold. We were giving O.S. Nock a day to remember and, after Chatham, I gave Les a break to Faversham. Between Chatham and Gillingham we were pulled up by signals on the viaduct and, as we were blowing off with a boiler of water, I left the fire alone through the tunnel while old Sam was pounding away. But when we left Gillingham the back end had gone and neither the pressure gauge nor the chimney top would show their appreciation of my efforts until we left Sittingbourne, by which time I had got that back end built up once more. Not only was I learning, for by no means the first nor last time, not to be clever but I also saw for myself the incredible power of the E1 when low in steam. What I had done and what I was seeing was exactly the same as the Battersea enginemen had learned over thirty years before. On the return, we had 1506 again and with the fire going down on the bars, we had to scheme a bit, and yet that old engine sailed up to Sole Street at 1 in 100 with less than 140psi and about 280 tons behind us and then tore down to Farningham Road at 77mph with the steam back to 130psi! Ossie Nock was amazed but there was far better in store, as we shall see.

Only once did I hear of one of our six to be in real trouble and that was on the Brighton side with the famous 18.10 Victoria - Uckfield which had ten bogies as far as Croydon and no banker out of No.17 platform. The 1 in 64 to the bridge could empty a boiler if the fire did not respond and, after Clapham Junction up to Balham, it was 1 in 93 and then a drag all the way. At the last moment, the booked Newhaven LM 4PT failed at the terminus and 1504 was rushed over to take its place. It should never have been sent, for it was overdue for a 'General' nor was the fire ready for a turn that had brought more than one Fairburn tank to its knees. The driver, in the Brighton Goods Link No.6, was an ex-LBSC man who had spent years in No.9, the 'Norwood Harriers' Link working W and C2X engines from Battersea Yard and I am sorry to say that when 1504 backed on, he was beaten before he started and they took an awful long time to get to Croydon and on to Oxted. As always, the shedmaster on the Southern took the rap for all the time lost by his engines and men so I got one on the knuckles for the use of an underpowered engine - and rightly so! As a result of this escapade, I was instructed to put 742 duty, the 18.10 turn, into the Brighton Passenger Link, despite the return working which was a freight from Horsham via the Mid Sussex, with a Stewarts Lane N 2-6-0.

What did my Battersea men think of the Converted Coppertops? Let us

As well as replacing various LBSC classes, the F1s and B1s took the place of the LCDR Kirtley bogies - class M3 - when they wor out in the late 'twenties. The James Stirling lineage is obvious but it was the Wainwright boiler with its extended smokebox tha made them so useful on secondary work. Photograph J. Tatchell Collection.

1031 arriving at Lewes from Eastbourne. The third rail is laid ready for electrification in 1935. At the same spot in 1933, a boy of ten looked longingly into the cab of an F1 and was invited to travel, to the amazement of his parents, with the crew to London Road, Brighton, a thrill I have never forgotten! Photograph J. Tatchell Collection.

sense of humour and a fine and conscientious engineman. Yes, he says, he had had 1749 one day last week and she was as good as when he was firing in the 'twenties and 'thirties. 'Cor, Guv', he said, 'they were wonderful jobs. We got 3d a day extra for firing them on boat trains when we were knocking about as spare men. But we never got mogadored with them!' Indeed, Percy never got *mogadored* with anything but he and his Fireman, Reg Wilks, gave O.S. Nock a day to remember on a 'King Arthur' on heavy relief boat trains in 1954. OSN subsequently wrote that he had never experienced more congenial company on a footplate nor seen a better exhibition of enginemanship.

Peter Wensley was an Old Kent Roader from the 'Brick' but he proved the point that the 'Converted Coppertops' as he still calls them, were truly firemen's engines. In 1956, about a year before Sammy Gingell retired in July 1957, he was working a special to Ramsgate with a rake of eight or nine old SECR 'Birdcage' coaches from London Bridge (LL) with a Stewarts Lane E1. Shortly before departure his fireman was taken ill and Bricklayers Arms rushed up a very young hand who had never been out on the road. Now quite a few senior drivers would have refused to take a greenhorn but nothing ever upset Sammy. With his usual smile, he welcomed the boy, young Peter, onto his footplate with 'Hello, Billy Boy, are you coming with me? Off we go then and all you need do is to put the coal just through that hole and I'll sort it out for you.' So within half a minute off they

stand on the front of Stewarts Lane shed one summer morning and see for ourselves. First of all, here comes Driver Harry Wing, normally quite cultured by our standards, but on this occasion he had a face of thunder and an acid tongue as he asks me what he is supposed to do with 'this thing'. indicating 1743 over his shoulder. He has 1743 for a Ramsgate, ten or eleven coaches on a duty which has been worked by a 'West Country' all the week but he would not have complained if I

had not been there. I know very well that he is simply making his point and that had I suggested that he might lose time with a Converted Coppertop, he would have been very indignant! Later the same morning, we have the smiling Percy Tutt with 1749. He had got her ready and saunters into the Foreman's office in search of a legpull and a cup of stewed tea. I ask him if he has had 1749 lately, as she is new out of Ashford. Now Percy is the archetypal Cockney, a lovely man with a great

Kirtley Bogie 647, by the old coal stage at Battersea. From the M3, the crack express engine of the LCDR was derived the D and the E and the hand of Surtees is clear. Photograph J. Tatchell Collection.

In the cab of the restored D No.737, Reg Wilks, then a young Stewarts Lane driver, stands on the fireman's side. Behind him is the regulator handle, the lubricator and by his left arm and in mid-gear, the Stirling reverser. The actual steam control valve to adjust the cut-off is forward of the reverser but out of sight. Photograph RHNH.

known Nine Elms driver, raconteur and author. But in 1944 he was still an unknown fireman, albeit a very good one. During the War, both classes were not unknown on the South Western side, as Stewarts Lane men worked the Victoria - Poole Harbour Pullman specials with their own engines, usually with ex-Nine Elms drivers such as Joe Brewer, 'Happy' Andrews and Syd Patrick, who needed but a refresher to know the way again. Old Sam got in on the act as well and probably learned the road in his spare time! However, in September 1941 five D1s were sent to Nine Elms and took over the work of the massive Drummond T14s, the 'Paddleboats', on the Basingstoke and Salisbury semi-fast services. Of course, the D1s were right hand drive and the Sou' West men had been used to the left hand side since Drummond arrived on the scene in 1897. So the engines not only appeared to be feeble little creatures in the eyes of No.2 Link but they were also cack handed, which did not go down too well at all.

But not for long! The ponderous T14s with their long, shallow, level grates were consigned to spare work and those Nine Elms men tore about with their economical 'Rebuilds' and how they enjoyed themselves riding their fiery little steeds which were booked to them on a regular double-manned basis, except for the very heaviest work in the link which would have been beyond the capability of a T14 in any case. Indeed they stayed at Nine Elms until 1945 before going back to the Eastern section. Now Bert Hooker was in the Mainline Pilot Gang at the time and well used to the engines and, one night, he was booked with a 42 year old Passed Fireman, Charlie Sutton, to work a troop train off the LNER from Canonbury to Fleet. As a U class was not available, they were given the D1 1145, one of those which were normally double manned and in very good

went, the 64 year old driver with the 16 year old boy. With Sam bent on regaining all time lost by the late start, 1019 roared past Peak Freans and attacked the old SER road climbing through Elmstead Woods to Chislehurst and then swung left at the junction for the ups and downs of the Chatham road. The boy had a job to stand up but he got the coal into the firebox now and again and kept at it, mile after mile. Sam, who loved to have his head over the side, (he once hit his head on the tunnel wall at Chatham which made him blink but no more) would reappear from time to time and look down at his little struggling stoker, ankle deep in coal and black as a sweep; 'How you doing, Billy Boy, ah, you're doing fine'. At Chatham and Faversham, Sam got coal down and filled the backend of the grate while 'Billy Boy' looked after the water and had a rest. No doubt Sam, who enjoyed firing as much as driving, gave him a blow from time to time on the road for Peter said that he was completely knackered by the time they got to Herne Bay. At Ramsgate they were relieved and soon caught a train home. Sam always bought his firemen a pint of 'Sherbert' as he called it but this time and in deference to the licensing laws, he bought Peter an ice cream! After all, the boy was only just 16 and hadn't started to grow for he was not much more than five feet tall. Besides, he was done in and Peter said, in later life, he never again worked so hard as the day he booked on for shed duty at the 'Brick' and found himself firing (though he did not know it at the time) to the legendary Sammy Gingell. But for a greenhorn who could never have reached the front of a long firebox, that steeply sloping grate and the heavy blast with old Sam hammering away

was a godsend, for the engine helped herself to coal where it was most needed. Perhaps this is not just a commentary on the temperament of an indomitable old man and a great hearted boy but also on their immensely capable little engine. As Sam so often said however hard the day, 'She's a good machine' or 'She's a marvel!'

We started with a memory of 1504 and 'Gramophone Edgeley' banking a West Country which could not restart, after a signal check on Sole Street bank, without assistance. 1504 never slipped and nor did 1145, a D1 and a very fine engine, on an even more remarkable occasion. Bert Hooker, who sadly died in the late May, needs no introduction these days as a well

O.S. Nock with Sammy Gingell at Swanley. Ossie wrote about this trip in glowing terms but it was but a pipe opener for what was to come later on the 11.50 Faversham, Duty 18.1504 had been cleaned by two ex-footplatemen who had been cleaning in the 'twenties and knew their business. She looked a picture. Photograph Author's Collection, the late John Click.

Driver Harry Wing in his last year of service, six years after our slight disagreement in the Foreman's office over the merits of 1743 for a ten coach Ramsgate. It could well be him, actually, firing on A179 at Battersea - see photo earlier. He would have been in Nos.1 or 2 link between 1924/29, first on the E1s then the Arthurs and finally on the Nelsons, all in those few years. Photograph Author's Collection, the late John Click.

give them a good shove out of Canonbury with the signalman passing the word that, on no account, should the train be checked until it had cleared Hampstead Heath tunnel. Bert had a tenderful of good hard coal and, at that time, 1145 had Ross Pop safety valves which did not lift until the pressure was right on the rated 180psi. The V2 gave them a good start for the length of the platform and then they were on the first stage of the climb. Bert says they settled down to about twelve miles per hour, in full forward gear and full regulator up the 1 in 87 with the boiler steaming perfectly. The engine accelerated to about 30mph on the easier grades to Camden Road and then swung right for the real trial of strength. Because of the curve and the load, they could not get much of a run at the 1 in 95. Absolutely flat out, the speed was held at about 15mph until they came to the curve at Gospel Oak, which brought them down a bit with just over half a mile to go. Between each steady spaced awesome crash of exhaust the Pop safety valves began to lift, before the next great gulp of steam through those 10in piston valves thrust the engine and its unwilling train forward up the grade with never a slip round Gospel Oak, on to Hampstead Heath and into the tunnel where they could give themselves and old 1145 a breather. What an engine and what railwaymen! Not for them a question of chucking in the towel and asking for assistance for, between them, they did the impossible and then worked through to Fleet, empties to

condition. It says a great deal for Nine Elms that they were able to maintain this practice in some links right through the War. Bert and his mate prepared 1145, took her light to Kensington and picked up their LMS pilotman for Canonbury, where they arrived at one o'clock in the morning.

They screwed the engine down and went to the signalbox for news of the trooper and a cup of tea and after a while it appeared with a 'Green Arrow' and fourteen corridor coaches, absolutely packed with soldiery and baggage. Here was a pretty kettle of fish and the LMS pilotman was very doubtful of the ability of so small an engine to master the load out of Canonbury and then up the fearsome climb to Hampstead Heath. The gradient at the start is 1 in 98, steepening to 1 in 87 and Bert suggested that the V2 should

The twinkling Percy Tutt in 1960, exactly as I knew him. I recently met one of his old firemen, Les Wood, who went into the Police. The happiest days of his working life were the two years he had in the Ramsgate link with Percy, a joy to come to work even at 03.00 on a winter's morning. Photograph RHNH.

I first met 'Billy Boy' when Major Peter Olver of the Railway Inspectorate asked me to vet the enginemen assigned to work the 'Iron Duke' in Hyde Park in 1985. What a fearsome thing it must have been in 1850. Peter Wensley is on the right, nearly 30 years after his epic day with old Sam. Mark Stutchbury is his stoker, both of them still on the railway. The Major, to whom railway preservation owes so much, has like me, 'Retired'. Photograph RHNH.

Basingstoke, turned and watered and home to Kensington with the empty stock. 500 tons and a 52 ton 4-4-0 express passenger engine with 6ft 8in driving wheels. The GN Atlantics were not the only engine to confound the theorists!

Now for the finale, in which 1019 and 1145 play their leading roles. Between 1952 and the later 'fifties, the 'Converted Coppertops' had their final fling on the SO 11.50 Faversham. Our No.2 Link had attracted a 'Fan Club' of timing specialists, Norman and Arthur Harvey and Syd Nash being very much to the fore and our men in their very different ways were only too pleased to oblige. In September 1956, some twenty one months after I had left the Southern for Stratford, it nevertheless fell to me to arrange for Peter Handford, then of Transacord, to travel in the front brake of the 11.50 to record for posterity the voice of 1019, the first of the 1920 E class rebuilds. Now it so happened that old Sam was on the job, with his regular mate, Jim Williams, and I went across to see that all went well. It did.

Jim Williams did the firing from Chatham and the driving to Chatham from Faversham with 1145. I fired to Sam from Victoria to Chatham and on the way back from Chatham to Bromley and then took the train up to Victoria. It was a day to remember. Sam started away from Victoria helped by a good banker, like a shot out of a gun - just listen to us on Peter's work of art! I put the left hand injector on when the Ramsbottom safety valves began to hum as we struck the 1 in 64 up to the bridge across the Thames. I suppose we had about 40% cut off and full regulator and you can hear the steam reverser pull the gear up to about 30% when we get onto the bridge. From time to time, I used the other feed to keep the boiler level con-

stant and to avoid blowing off steam as we roared up to Nunhead and with a lurch, swung right for Catford. For Peter's benefit, we were banging on a bit and so we were checked at Bickley and before Swanley, probably by the 11.35 from Victoria which had stopped at Bromley and had been proceeding uphill in a more decorous manner.

However, we were up to 50mph by Swanley before we began our headlong dash for Farningham Road, the engine vibrating with life and energy as it tore up to 80 down the gradient. Jim and I stood on our respective sides of the cab whilst Sam, with his head outside, was oblivious to everything except the task of doing what had never been done before, not even in the 'twenties. After Farningham the grade changes abruptly to 1 in 100 and Sam reappeared to juggle with the Stirling steam reverser to lengthen the cut-off before the speed fell away. What happened then, we shall never know, for the gear went full forward and for a couple of seconds, our world went mad. Without a word, Sam got the lever where

Sam's last run on a 'Converted Coppertop', the D1 31545, at Margate with his trusty mate, Jim Williams, after working the 90 minute SLS special in 1957. The Inspector would not allow Jim to work with the usual fire and much of the run was made with low steam pressure. Sam did not like this and would not directly oppose the inspector - but he had his methods. The train flew through Westgate at 70 mph, Margate was sighted and Sam closed the regulator gently and applied the vacuum brake fully. Entering the station at some 50 mph he carefully placed the brake handle in the 'running' position, never touched it again and stopped exactly right for water at the column. Genius or luck? Old Sam just grinned and said he knew what he was doing! Photograph R.C. Bending.

Uphill and just as it should be with the stop at Bromley not far away. Not a sign of smoke or steam on a coolish day. Nor a safety valve, gland or injector. Nobody in sight. We were helping our little marvel, 1145 to do what should have been impossible. *Que de souvenir imperissable!* Photograph Monsieur R.C. Riley.

he wanted it but my fire, built up high at the back of the grate and filling the firehole, disappeared with the long uphill stretch ahead of us. Listen to the record and you will hear that fearful roar of an engine going into full gear with full regulator at 80mph but then you will marvel at the climb to Meopham and Sole Street which follows.

When the fire went down the slope and up against the tubeplate, there was only one solution and there were two of us there to do the job. Lumps, the bigger the better off the tender top, passed by hand and placed under the firehole door to rebuild the backend, one after another, no time to waste and with hands, boots and shovel, the job was done and a desperate situation avoided. Sam never fussed or worried but as he knew that what was needed was being done, he paid not the slightest attention. But the old engine did, the 175psi became a rock-like 140 but she roared through Meopham and then topped Sole Street at an incredible 60 up the 1 in 132, a 52 ton locomotive with at least 280 tons on her tail. Listen to the record and wonder how on earth it could be done with steam 40psi below the working pressure. Then it was over - for a few minutes - until we were checked near the Medway bridge and had to accelerate through Rochester and then again before the tunnel to bring us into Chatham, more than a few minutes early. Again, listen to the acceleration, the echo of the exhaust against the buildings we passed and imagine old Sam, as happy as a sandboy, enjoying every minute of it. And so did Jim and I.

At Faversham we were relieved by Dover men. We went across the road taking Peter and his equipment with us but sadly he had to return on an earlier train and so missed what was probably the most amazing piece of work ever achieved by a Rebuild. For some reason the booked 1749 did not

turn up with the 14.02 ex-Dover Priory and we knew nothing about 1145, a Dover engine. The train was late arriving and the Dover men had little to say, often a good sign: the coal was the usual soft Kentish mixture of Snowdown or Chislet, sometimes an unknown quantity. We did well to Chatham but were still five minutes down when we left. We had plenty of steam as we attacked Sole Street bank starting so we were told, at 39mph. But we had a marvellous machine, for the harder Sam worked her the better she steamed, not using a great deal of coal or water whilst the pressure rose to the full 180psi as the speed gradually increased to 42 mph with 280 tons up 1 in 100. We couldn't believe it and we stood there, with the firehole door open, fearing some terrible priming brought on by the free steaming, was about to start.

But we kept the backend of the fire right up to the top of the firehole and once over the top, Sam, who had been waiting for just such a situation, wound our old engine and its eight coach train up to an incredible 87mph, not on a long down grade where it could be done gradually but an 87 with every exhaust beat sharp and clear above the deafening racket within the cab. Swanley stopped us, just and with a jerk, but our blood was up and the photograph taken by Dick Riley must be the final compliment to the Maunsell Rebuild. It was not a warm day, we were going uphill and yet there was no smoke, not a breath of steam showing at chimney top, at safety valve, at gland or injector. There was nobody in sight on the footplate for we were working parts of our little machine. The three of us had helped her to do what should have been quite impossible.

So my memories of these wonderful engines will always be with me. What a tragedy that one was not saved from the scrapyard to keep the legend alive. But there it is. One thinks of them go-

ing over the arches above Stewarts Lane, running into Victoria with a job well done, dropping down into the Lane, mid-morning, from Factory Junction off one of the two day duties. We often got the Bricklayers Arms engines in the summer and there was 1497 with a taller chimney, as fitted to the original 'River' tanks. I stood near her one day, talking to the crew, at the buffer stops at Victoria before she banked her train. The right away was given, the regulator was opened full first port and those long rocking arms, in full back gear, started to swing back and forth with the rhythm of a University Eight. And, under the station roof, that marvellous exhaust bark which made the blood quicken. A 52 ton quart in a pint pot, just a 'Converted Coppertop' but thanks to Peter's recording, I shall always be able to hear the voice of 1019 so that I can relive that day in 1956. The sounds and the memories of the men and machines bring tears of joy and emotion to my eyes.

Note:
Books consulted during my delvings into the background of the Converted Coppertops were:- Locomotives of R.E.L. Maunsell *by O.S. Nock, pub. Edward Everard;* Locomotive Adventure Vols 1 and 2, *particularly Vol 2, by H. Holcroft, pub. Ian Allan;* Locomotives of the SER, Locomotives of the SECR, Locomotives of the LCDR, *all by D.L. Bradley, pub. RCTS.*
Mogadored. *To be* mogadored *was to be messed up, buggered up and seriously short of steam and water, maybe having to stop for a blowup. Mogador was a Cockney/Gypsy word and also the name of a telephone exchange in the rather classy Kingswood, Burgh Heath, Tadworth area! It is not in the OED but could well be in the comparable book of slang. It was used a lot by the older south Londoners - Battersea, Old Kent Road, Walworth, Kennington, Peckham, New Cross, Deptford - the purer Cockney strains...*

GRANTHAM
Hub of the Great Northern

2556 ORMONDE north of Potters Bar on the 5.30pm King's Cross to Newcastle, a Grantham working, on which it would go through to York. This timing dates the picture as being taken prior to September 1935 when the Silver Jubilee began to run at this time. It has long travel valves which were fitted in November 1930, after it had moved to Grantham in June 1928, where it stayed for ten years. This shows the usual high polish found on Grantham engines although it has been in traffic for six hours and through sixteen tunnels!

By Eric Neve

Joining the Great Northern Railway at Grantham in 1902, Bill Carman was a cleaner until 1906 and after 14 years was promoted to driver in 1920. Proceeding through the various links, he was in No.2 Passenger Link in 1935, when Atlantic No.3275 was his booked engine; he was promoted to No.1 Link in 1937, taking over Pacific No.4479 from F. Coy. It fell to Driver Carman's lot to take the heaviest known passenger train out of King's Cross, on 5th April 1940, when the 1.00pm departure was made up to no fewer than 25 bogie coaches *weighing 750 tons tare, 850 tons full.* It was loaded in two parts in separate platforms and when these were joined, the huge formation stretched well into Gasworks Tunnel. Whether or not it was assisted by the tank engine at the rear (which had brought in the empty stock) is not recorded but it took sixteen minutes to clear Finsbury Park, two and a half miles away. After that A4 No.2509 SILVER LINK ran the ensuing 103 miles to Grantham in 123 minutes. Despite this remarkable achievement, eleven minutes were booked against the engine. After changing crews at Grantham the famous A4 went on to Newcastle, losing only four minutes.

In the 1948 Locomotive Exchanges, driver Carman was detailed to conduct the LMR driver with Royal Scot No.46146, working the 7.50am test train ex-Leeds from Grantham to King's Cross. The train was running a little late but the driver was imbued

by the need to reach London on time. Passing Peterborough, where there was a strict 20mph speed restriction, there was some altercation between the LMR driver and his ER conductor and speed was not reduced sufficiently - so that it was a miracle the train did not derail while traversing the severe curves. Driver Carman was so upset by this that on arrival in London, he went straight to Liverpool Street to see the Locomotive Running Superintendent, G.A. Musgrave, asking to be relieved from further duties on the test runs later that week. I chanced to meet Driver Carman that day as he returned

to King's Cross and he told me the story. For the remaining runs with No.46146 Grantham deputed Driver Morris as conductor; he told me he had no trouble, but was not saying too much!

Whilst A4s were shedded at Grantham, Bill Carman became attached to No.6 (60006). One day in those very unhappy times about 1950, Top Shed (Kings Cross) was having difficulty in finding engines for their booked turns. The station loco foreman, Tom Taylor, was bewailing his lot in front of enginemen in the mess room until Bill could stand it no longer. In

2549 PERSIMMON is approaching New Southgate, un-named, in an early LNER livery with the number on the tender - placed on the cab in May 1928. It was transferred from Doncaster to Grantham in July 1927 (when it was fitted with long travel valves) for a fifteen year spell. The train, having three non-corridor coaches (as well as two brake vans) at its head, barely qualifies for Class A express category - it is more likely to be empty stock on transfer.

2545 DIAMOND JUBILEE at King's Cross shed, in an early LNER livery - the number on the tender was placed on the cab in May 1928. 2545 also had the early short travel valves. At the time of the photograph, it was a King's Cross engine, and moved to Grantham in June 1928, where it stayed for fifteen years. During its time at King's Cross it was used as the 'home' engine in the loco exchange trials with the GWR Castle 4079 in May 1925 when, for reasons not fully recorded its performance, after it was substituted for the original candidate, was less than satisfactory. It lost 50 minutes on five return trips (three to and from Grantham and two to and from Doncaster to King's Cross) and used just under 4lb of coal per mile more than the Castle. In the light of the later figure, long travel valves were fitted to all A1s, and later A3s and A4s; this was successful in cutting coal consumption and lead, in later years, to the Pacifics' superiority over the Castle in this important matter.

2549 PERSIMMON near Greenwood Box on an up express. The engine was transferred to Grantham in July 1927 (when it was fitted with long travel valves) for fifteen years. The stock includes two non-corridor and two elderly pre-Gresley coaches next to the engine, suggesting that it was the 8.30am, which started from Grantham and stopped at Essendine, Little Bytham, Peterborough and Huntingdon en route to London. The leisurely schedule did not justify a top link Pacific on this leg but the return working (the heavy 1.15pm Edinburgh) provided the justification for such motive power.

his younger days he had done relief duties as Running Foreman at Grantham and announced to Tom, "You're only a one-way shed, working northwards and you don't know what trouble is! At Grantham we work *four* ways - north, south, east and west". This little episode inspired the title of my article. The present offering is not intended as a detailed history of Grantham shed but an attempt to highlight the achievements of that little-publicised institution.

Railway life at Grantham began in 1850 when the Ambergate Railway line from Nottingham was opened and a small engine shed built by Grantham canal. It was replaced by a larger shed opposite the station in 1855. Meanwhile, in 1852, the GNR had opened their 'Towns Line' from Werrington to Retford via Grantham and Newark and built their own station at Grantham. For a decade no GN engines were based there, as Peterborough, Retford, Doncaster and occasionally even Newark, had been established as changing points. With the coming of larger locomotives Patrick Stirling was anxious to increase the length of their runs and to facilitate this, water columns were installed at Peterborough station in 1862, so that engines could run the 105 and a half miles between London and Grantham without recourse to a shed. The GNR built one not far from the Ambergate building and allocated engines to this Grantham shed in 1862. A second building was put up a little further south in 1896, by which time Grantham had become a focal point on the system, with its engines working west to Nottingham, Derby, Stafford and Leicester, north to York, east to Lincoln and Boston and south to London.

No details of the earliest engine complement at Grantham are available but from 1868 onwards Stirling 7ft 2-2-2s of the 41 - 61 series were there. From 1870 Stirling 8ft 6ins 2-4-0s would have been there for working the branches, along with mixed traffic 0-4-2s. Three of the earliest Stirling 6ft singles 2, 3 and 5, went there in 1871/73 for use on the best express work to London and York. By 1895 there were seventeen eight footers on the Grantham strength and it was with these that the shed first came under notice, particularly on the 'Manchester Fliers' of 1880, which they ran to London and back. The high standards

Left:- 2557 BLAIR ATHOL on an up express south of Hatfield post-May 1931 when long travel valves were fitted. The train is hard to identify and while it is said to be from Edinburgh, the evidence of the late afternoon light and the mixed look of the stock, does not support this. (ECML trains always had the best stock). One of the first A1s to go to Grantham, 2557 arrived in March 1925 after a month running-in at Gorton on the GC. It stayed for 17 years. The clean livery is a credit to the shed staff and to Driver F. Sharpe, the regular driver in the late 1930s.

2558 TRACERY climbing in Saltersford cutting en route from Grantham to Stoke summit, the corridor but non-streamlined tender indicating the time to be post-June 1937. The train was probably the 1.10pm from Leeds and 2558 had just taken over at Grantham. The engine returned on the 7.25pm Aberdonian and this explains why it is carrying a reversed headboard on the middle lamp iron, ready for use on the second leg of the diagram.

2560 PRETTY POLLY. This can be accurately identified since the print used is an original produced by George Grigs, a founder of the RCTS and the card is now in the FAS collection. He says it shows the 1.40pm from King's Cross just north of Potters Bar on Tuesday 15th March 1938. 2560 went to Grantham in November 1928 and stayed for fourteen years, during which (January 1930) it received long travel valves. The 1.40pm stopped at Peterborough, Grantham, Newark, Retford (portion for Sheffield), Doncaster, (portion for Harrogate plus the restaurant car - the LNER knew how to win brownie points!) and Selby, with the engine working right through to York. The train terminated at Newcastle, a journey of 6hrs 24mins.

set by Drivers Hall, Hawbrook, Lamb, Knight and Silkstone were praised by the recorder Chas. Rous-Marten. In the 1888 'Race to Edinburgh' No.775 achieved the best run from Grantham to York, averaging 59.1 miles per hour, despite checks amounting to six minutes. Seven years later during the 'Race to Aberdeen' driver Lamb with the same engine covered the 82.7 miles to York in 76 minutes - an average of 65.3 mph and a record unbeaten until 1916. From 1898 the 8 foot singles began to be displaced by Ivatt's 'Klondyke' Atlantics of which seven were based at Grantham including the first one, No.990 HENRY OAKLEY. It was said the District Loco Superintendent refused to roster that engine to the best duties, in deference to his allegiance to the Stirling Singles!

After only six years in office Ivatt brought out his finest design, the large Atlantics of which in time sixteen were based at Grantham, thereby giving a stud of 23 4-4-2s and hastening the demise of the Singles. By 1913 all 94 large Atlantics were in service and gradually Grantham acquired 23 of them, so that the smaller 'Klondykes' could be moved away for less exacting duties. Before that happened No.982 on the up 'Flying Scotsman', weighing 490 tons gross, reached King's Cross unaided in 135 minutes (four minutes early) for the 105.5 miles (average 46.9 mph) including a maximum of 77.5 mph at Essendine; a sterling effort by an engine of that size with nearly 500 tons. Large Atlantic No.1404 took 146 minutes net with 590 tons (average 43.4 mph). Such heavy loads worked unaided were typical of the effort made by Grantham men during the 1914/18 war.

Two very special trains ran from King's Cross on 4th June 1916 in connection with a journey taken by Lord Kitchener, then Secretary of State for War, and his staff en route to Scotland on what proved their last journey before the warship they were on was sunk by enemy action. The first train of four bogies (100/110 tons) was taken out of London by 'Klondyke'

Left:- 4476 ROYAL LANCER is leaving King's Cross on an afternoon train which can be identified by the stock as it is not the usual rake of bogie vehicles. The first five cars are non-corridors with ample toilet facilities which suggests that the train is made up of several portions to be split - Hitchin for East Anglia, maybe, and Peterborough for the M&GN and Lincolnshire. The 3.00pm was such a train with through facilities to Cambridge and to Wisbech, King's Lynn, Cromer, Sheringham and finally Boston, hence the need for the rash of destination headboards which are to be found on all the coaches. Why a Pacific was required for this unimportant train on which it ran only to Peterborough, is hard to determine unless it was required for the second leg of the diagram which called for such a large loco. Even the reason for the train can be seriously questioned as all the destinations could be easily reached by alternative routes - especially Cromer.

4476 ROYAL LANCER in Salterford cutting climbing five miles at 1/200 en route to Stoke Summit on an up express. It was allocated to Grantham from new in 1923 until April 1928 when it went to works for a general repair and was transferred to King's Cross with one of the first corridor tenders, for the then-new 'Non-Stop' to Edinburgh. In July 1937 this was replaced by a new high-sided but non-corridor tender so the picture was taken when 4476 was allocated to King's Cross. The strangely dirty tender is also a give-away to the allocation of 4476 as it would have been unlikely to have escaped the eagle eye of the Grantham shed foreman!

4478 HERMIT on an up express at the south end of Welwyn Viaduct. It was shedded at Grantham for nearly ten years from September 1928 and received long-travel valves in April 1930. Judging by the angle of the sunlight, it is likely to be on the 1.10pm from Leeds due at King's Cross at 5.05pm and 4478 will have taken over at Grantham possibly with Driver A.C. Hall at the regulator, as this was his regular engine in the late 1930s.

Duties undertaken by No.1 Link from June 1925:		
Dep.	To	Return
5.12am	King's Cross	10am Flying Scotsman
8.30am	King's Cross	1.15pm Edinburgh
11.30am	King's Cross	5.30pm Newcastle
3.10pm	King's Cross	7.30pm Aberdonian
5.18pmSX	King's Cross	10.25pmSX Night Scotsman
6.21pm	King's Cross	11.30pm express Goods
12.7pm	York	2.31pm Up Flying Scotsman
3.23pm	York (Edinburgh)	6.15pm Up Afternoon Scotsman
7.31pm	York (Newcastle)	1.5am Up Newcastle Sleeper
9.31pm	York (perth)	3.24am Up Edinburgh Sleeper

No.252 and reached Grantham in 117 minutes (average 54 mph). Onwards, large Atlantic No.284, manned by driver Short and fireman Carman suffered a four minute delay through track repairs and lost ten minutes through adverse signals at Doncaster, thus taking 108 minutes to York (94 minutes net = 52.6 mph). Some important documents were left behind in London, making a second train necessary. Hurriedly arranged, this consisted of only two coaches hauled by the King's Cross main line pilot, Atlantic No.1442 which reached Grantham in 101 minutes - average 62.6 mph (Hatfield to Peterborough = 70.5mph). Thence Ivatt Superheated 4-4-0 No.57, with driver R. Robinson and fireman A. Skerritt, passed Doncaster, 50.5 miles, in 45 minutes (average 67.3 mph) but were heavily delayed after that by a North Eastern train ahead, to the extent of 18 minutes. York was

reached in 97 minutes (69 minutes net = average 71.7 mph). Both firemen personally assured me 30 years later that they were concerned in those events despite other names being published.

Ivatt 4-4-0s, both saturated and superheated, undertook a lot of work between Grantham and York, particularly on the 2.20pm Scotsman from King's Cross. Just how hard these duties were for firemen were made clear to me. In their words one fired all the way from Grantham to Chaloners Whin (just south of York) and then from York to Peascliff tunnel (just north of Grantham) coming home!

By Grouping in 1923, Grantham's allocation of express engines included 33 large Atlantics, with weekday duties on nine return trips to London, four to York and one

to Doncaster, shared between No.1 and No.2 links in which drivers normally had their own regular engines. The second link also included turns to Lincoln, Boston, Derby and Stafford. At peak periods a good number of additional duties were undertaken both to London and York.

Of the first twelve Gresley Pacifics, Grantham received three, ex-Doncaster Works between May and August 1923. They were Nos.4476, 4479 and 4480, later to be named in 1925/26 ROYAL LANCER, ROBERT THE DEVIL and ENTERPRISE; they operated the heaviest turns to London and York but were not booked to regular drivers at that time. By April 1925 seven more Pacifics had been allocated

A1 PACIFICS ALLOCATED TO GRANTHAM, APRIL 1925			
DATE	LOCO	DRIVER	DISPLACED LARGE ATLANTIC
5/23	4476 ROYAL LANCER	R. Chatwin	3261
7/23	4479 ROBERT THE DEVIL	H. Doolan	4432
8/23	4480 ENTERPRISE	L. Wright	4448
8/24	2547 DONCASTER	Sarratt	4417
9/24	2548 GALTEE MORE	Mills	4405
2/25	2550 BLINK BONNY	H. Hall	4443
2/25	2551 PRINCE PALATINE	T. Short	3296
2/25	2566 ORMONDE	T. Baines	4436
3/25	2567 BLAIR ATHOL	F. Sharpe	3294
4/25	2568 TRACERY	R. Robinson	4414

4479 ROBERT THE DEVIL on an up Newcastle express in the favourite position of Frank Hebron, late post-master of Balcombe, Sussex - that is, just south of Ganwick box which was replaced by an early installation of colour lights on the ECML in the summer of 1932 - control passing (from the south) to Greenwood Box and Potters Bar box to the north. The signal cables can be seen just below the buffer beam on the up side. The train is composed largely of nearly new end-door stock and could well be the 'Junior Scotsman' a name given to the 10.10am relief from Edinburgh, as its make up so nearly replicates that of the Flying Scotsman. This poses the now-unanswerable question as to why a Grantham A1 is hauling an ECML train when their London turns were almost entirely on trains from the West Riding. 4479 came new to Grantham shed in July 1923 and by staying there throughout the post-war years, the 'fence squatters' who watched the daily movements on the main line came to consider it to be the archetypal Lincolnshire based A1

Last Days at Grantham 1. V2 2-6-2 No.60848 of Darlington shed, under the coaling plant at Grantham, 24th April 1960. Photograph J.F. Aylard.

Last Days at Grantham 2. Kings Cross V2, 60854, on down empty coaching stock passing Grantham station on 16th April 1963, only six months before its withdrawal. No doubt its arrival was preceded by the usual message to waiting passengers from the lady announcer - *"Please stand back as this train is not stopping here"*. The smokebox door handle of 60854 has been modified, as it is in two sections - only six locos bore this feature. Photograph M.S. Castledine.

enabling the ten Top Link drivers to have their regular ones, giving up their cherished Atlantics. On Saturdays the 5.10pm to London was worked by King's Cross as the 10.25pm from London did not run. The Grantham crew worked to Lincoln and back, arriving there at 8.19pm and returning at 10.05pm. This enabled the top link to retain their route knowledge to Lincoln, should the main line be blocked. The foregoing notes were compiled by Mr. G.N. Everett of Lincoln and kindly given to me by Mr D. Jackson.

In those times there were no 'rest days'; 150 miles equalled a day's work for the crew and every 15 miles over 150 equalled 1 hours pay, so men working six return trips to London made 28 hours 30 minutes in mileage pay. York turns made fourteen and a half hours a week, so earnings were quite good at that period. A contemporary report in *The Railway Magazine* stated that locomotive working from King's Cross to York and back with the Flying Scotsman trains was inaugurated in 1924 and it has been wrongly assumed this was by King's Cross shed. This was not so, as can be seen from the foregoing table. Grantham was responsible for working the 10.00am from London through to York and after a hurried turnround the enginemen involved went back only to Grantham with the up train. Similar duties involved the 1.15pm and 5.30pm trains from King's Cross and in all three cases engines would go through from London to York. In May 1928 introduction of the non-stop 'Flying Scotsman' to Edinburgh took the 10.00 duty away from Grantham, but they retained the other two turns.

A notable Grantham No.2 'Atlantic' Link duty was the 7.40pm goods from Grantham to Colwick followed by the 11.35pm Milk (10.15pm ex-Egginton Jct.) to King's Cross. This was non-stop over the 125.2 miles Netherfield (Nottingham) to Finsbury Park in 185 minutes. For some time this was the longest all year non-stop run on the GN section. From early in the 1930s the same link also ran the 10.10am ex-King's Cross through to Leeds, taking over from No.1 link at Grantham. Return from Leeds was on the 3.07pm. In times of pressure it was known for one engine to work the 5.12am Grantham - King's Cross; then the 10.10am to Leeds, return to London and finally back to Grantham on the 10.25pm 'Night Scotsman' - just short of 600 miles in under 24 hours. It is not clear when a Grantham A1 first regularly worked through from Doncaster to Leeds on the 10.10am from Kings Cross. Records show that through working was taking place by 31st December 1934, the earliest date traced so far, but it is known that double heading of an A1 by a smaller engine was authorised* by November 1933. So a single A1 would almost certainly have been *regularly* allowed before this, possibly from May 1932 when

Last Days at Grantham 3. Copley Hill's A1 ABBOTSFORD on Saturday 1st June 1963, on an up express for London. Judging by the long shadows and the passenger on the up platform shielding his eyes from the low sun, this could be the 5.15pm Saturdays Only from Harrogate, due away at 8.35pm and timed to arrive at Kings Cross at 10.20pm. Photograph M.S. Castledine.

great changes took place in train schedules and the introduction of more lodging turns between London and Newcastle, thus depriving Grantham of their work on the 1.15 and 5.30pm from London. Under the revised workings, the top link undertook six return trips to London and four to York each week. Seven of the trains were heavy night sleeping car formations and only three duties were what the men regarded as 'day jobs' - the others were all at night.

In 1934 the milk train ceased to run non-stop between Netherfield and Finsbury Park but Grantham still worked it from there and returned with the 4.45am express from King's Cross. This was usually loaded to about 450 tons, so a second Atlantic would be required to assist. Often another Grantham engine and crew was used, which had come up on a double headed meat train assisting a King's Cross engine. Thus on 27th June 1935 the 4.45am was hauled by No.4405 (Driver Bott) who had assisted No.4461 (Driver W.Sheen of King's Cross) on the

(see page 32)The first occasion on which a Pacific worked through from King's Cross to Leeds was on the West Riding Pullman on May 15th 1930. This was arranged in order that an A1 would be available to work the up Pullman to London on 16th March, when two extra coaches were to be added for an important French Delegation. This one-off working did not mark the start of regular through work by Pacifics.

up meat train and No.3296 (Driver A.C. Hall who had worked the up milk train). Naturally the lineside observers did not often see these early morning trains!

Grantham links came into their own on busy summer Saturdays, as on 13th July when, in addition to the six No.1 link turns to London, no fewer than twelve were also handled by No.2 link. Of the fourteen Pacifics allocated to Grantham in 1937, ten were in No.1 link with regular drivers, as follows:-

2545 DIAMOND JUBILEE (Bottomley)
2548 GALTEE MORE (Taylor)
2549 PERSIMMON (Schofield)
2550 BLINK BONNY (Skerritt)
2554 WOOLWINDER (A.Southwell)
2558 TRACERY (Wellbourne)
2560 PRETTY POLLY (G.W. Hall)
2562 ISINGLASS (Pearson)
4478 HERMIT (A.C. Hall)
4479 ROBERT THE DEVIL (W.Carman)

The two brothers Hall were the last of the family to work on the footplate and were distinguished members of the Grantham top link. The association had begun with 'Old father Hall' who had driven Stirling Singles, and as well as G.W. and A.C. mentioned above another son, Harry, was in the link until the early 1930s. Pity the shedmaster who had to keep track of that trio! By August 1939 the only changes were that No.2557 BLAIR ATHOL had replaced HERMIT; 2750 PAPYRUS (Grantham's first A3) and 2551 PRINCE PALATINE had replaced 2558 TRACERY and 2562 ISINGLASS

respectively. Driver Tindall and Hollingworth replaced Southwell and Wellbourne respectively. Benny Tindall was very proud of his WOOLWINDER which he dosed with a personal mixture of oil. When the engine went to Plant, the Grantham District Loco Supt. received a special request inquiring why there was so little wear in the bearings!

The first A4s to be allocated to the shed were Nos.4466 HERRING GULL and 4494 OSPREY in April 1938, to cover a new long diagram on the down 'Aberdonian', to Edinburgh and back next evening on the up 'Night Scotsman', but not with specific crews. Changes during the war took many more streamliners to Grantham including Nos.2509 SILVER LINK, 4468 MALLARD, 4495 GOLDEN FLEECE and 4496 GOLDEN SHUTTLE. Inevitably the established practice of regular engines on duties went by the board in wartime and train schedules varied from year to year. Loadings often exceeded 20 bogies and Grantham men had their full share of these huge formations. When the milk trains were reduced to just one, Grantham lost its overnight turn to London; King's Cross then had to work the early express around 4.00am to Grantham, returning with the erstwhile 'Mark Lane Express' (so named from its use by corn merchants and farmers attending weekly markets held in Mark Lane, near the Tower of London) which had been a Grantham preserve since its inception in January 1889. From 1932 to 1939 it had been the fastest sched-

Last Days at Grantham 4. A3 60061 PRETTY POLLY of Kings Cross standing at the north end of Grantham station on a down express in April 1963, only moths before its withdrawal. Note the ex-GC 'Barnum' coach in the sidings. Photograph M.S. Castledine.

uled run for them, covering the 58.9 miles from Huntingdon to King's Cross in 58 minutes at 60.9 mph. The drivers were naturally most aggrieved at this loss but were partially mollified by getting the Leeds 'Breakfast Flier', as Doncaster men did not work south of Peterborough in wartime. Sometimes they had to bring through V2s working from Leeds to London. The fires would be in a very dirty state and time was lost in consequence. However, instead of suffering a bad return journey on the 1.50pm down they would put the engine over the pit in the loco yard at King's Cross, rake out all the clinker, take coal and get a good fire going before a well earned rest and going home without trouble. By no means would men from some other depots do that!

There was one well remembered day when I looked in vain for the Grantham men in King's Cross station to take the 1.50pm down. Eventually they emerged from Gasworks tunnel with a nondescript V2 and coupled on. Instead of coming over to have their customary chat with me, Driver Pinchbeck and Fireman Roger Hunt busied themselves on the footplate until Roger could stand it no longer. Coming down on to the platform he whispered in my ear "We've run BLINK BONNY [2550] hot." "You'll be for it at home then" I replied.

Two unreported events were related to me by the drivers concerned. Bob Dodd took the 'Night Scotsman' to York

on that fateful night of 28th/29th April 1942 when the coaches were set alight by incendiaries, while standing in the station. The crew protected themselves by crouching between the platform wall and their engine! This was the night A4 No.4469 (see BRILL 2.5) suffered terminal bomb damage in York shed. Driver Healey later told me how he had worked the train conveying Russia's Foreign Minister, Molotov, who had landed at a northern port. The train stopped at Brookmans Park (near Hatfield) where Molotov disembarked, to be whisked by car across quiet country roads to meet the British Government at Chequers, in Buckinghamshire.

In October 1943 I was able to obtain details of the Grantham Top Link, which still had ten crews - Skerritt, Hollingworth, W. Carman, A.C. Hall, Tindall, Healey, Pinchbeck, Jarvis, J. Dodd, G.W. Hall. They had six turns to London, two to York, one to Lincoln and Main Line Pilot (held in reserve for failures). No longer did they have the 'Flying Scotsman' which had been altered to stop at Peterborough but it was worked there by King's Cross men and onwards to York by a New England crew. This was not to the liking of Grantham, where the loss of such a prestige job was keenly resented. However, in 1946 the Peterborough stop was omitted in favour of Grantham whence their men took the train to York. The record of New England had not been impressive on the duty and

Grantham were determined to ensure they did better. No matter how late the 'Scotsman' might be on the takeover at Grantham it became the tradition to get back on time by York. By then the Grantham drivers had taken to getting A4s as regularly as possible. In particular Jarvis had SEAGULL and he never tired of telling me he would go out and beat MALLARD's record given the chance!

The winter service of 1948/9 was received by Grantham with unrestrained elation, for not only did they get a through turn to Newcastle on the 'Flying Scotsman', the job was one *regained* from King's Cross. The full working was to take the 'Night Scotsman' to London, then the 10.00am Scotsman as far as Grantham, to be replaced there by a fresh engine and crew to Newcastle, who went back home on the afternoon Scotsman with a Gateshead A4, leaving their own engine to return during the night to Grantham. Crews worked the duty alternate days to Newcastle. Two Pacifics were nominated for these jobs, working alternate days to King's Cross and to Newcastle, thus totalling 2,238 miles weekly. At first A3 No.60039 SANDWICH and A4 60030 GOLDEN FLEECE served in an unbroken spell from 27th September until 12th November 1948, when the engines were changed for A4s 60007 SIR NIGEL GRESLEY and 60008 DWIGHT D. EISENHOWER. Pride in the job was unbounded. The engines were kept spotlessly clean and

Last Days at Grantham 5. O2 63987 on up ore empties from Frodingham (bound for the ironstone quarry sidings in the High Dyke area) passing the north end of the up platform on 16th April 1963. It is strange that the gas lamp remains despite the arrival of a new electric lamp standard - belt and braces maybe? Note the telegraph pole which carried the control phone/telegraph circuits, and backbone of the ECML. Woe betide anyone who managed to demolish one with a heavy shunt... Photograph M.S. Castledine.

Last Days at Grantham 6. New England V2 No.60950 of New England approaching the station from the north on 1st January 1963, on a short twenty wagon fast fitted freight. Though the loco was last in works in May 1962 (*Yeadon's Register Vol 4*, Irwell Press, 1992) it is in spanking clean condition for a New England V2 - they usually looked very neglected a few months out of works. Photograph M.S. Castledine.

nonetheless, to work through with other shed's engines to London, York and Newcastle. This scheme proved an utter disaster and lasted only until September 1951, when Chief Inspector J ('Sam') Jenkins was charged with the task of restoring some order to the situation. All nineteen Southern Area A4s plus the W1 were based at King's Cross and Grantham received a stud of A1s; 60113, 60122, 60128, 60130, 60131, 60136, 60148, 60149, 60156, 60157 and 60158, all from King's Cross. There were then twelve crews in the Top Link sharing six A1s, thus:-

60122 CURLEW Drivers Jarvis and Walton.
60128 BONGRACE Drivers Healey and Brownsell.
60131 OSPREY Drivers Atterton and Barnes.
60149 AMADIS Drivers Measures and Marshall.
60156 GREAT CENTRAL Drivers Thompson and Taylor.
60113 GREAT NORTHERN Drivers Ross and Hudson.

Thereafter other changes occurred gradually but Grantham did not house any diesel express locomotives. The end of a century's distinguished service to the East Coast main line came on 7th September 1963 when the shed was closed.

Readers may be interested to know that some months before he died in October 1992, Eric Neve passed me the manuscript for this article and asked if I would see if a magazine might be found to publish it. Needless to say, it was eagerly accepted at BRILL and I would like to thank the Editor for finding space for Eric's last article, which is on one of his favourite subjects - the rosters of engines and men at the old GNR depots.

John Aylard, 1995.

Last Days at Grantham 7. An original Great Northern gas lamp on the down platform in April 1959, with a first-generation (then new) DMU standing at the down platform, waiting to leave for Nottingham or Lincoln. The shadow pattern on the coach roof is intriguing as the source is not immediately obvious - the roof is tiled as far as can be seen. Strange to think that the diesel coach also followed the lamp into oblivion some years ago. *Tempus fugit.*

mechanically sound. Each day at Grantham the Shedmaster and Mechanical Foreman were present on the platform to see off their engines to Newcastle. The tradition then became for the famous train to be on time at Newcastle, come what may in the shape of checks.

When non-stop running between London and Edinburgh was restored in the summer of 1949, the Grantham A4 booked for the 10.00 down Scotsman stood pilot for the 'Capitals Limited'. Returning from overhaul early in November 1949 A4 60030 GOLDEN FLEECE went onto the Newcastle duty on 29th and remained thereon continuously until 7th April 1950. Eighteen weeks of running, 40,284 miles without trouble, highlighted the dedication of Grantham's staff and restored faith in Gresley's Pacifics. At the same

time the Grantham Shedmaster decided to keep the veteran 60106 FLYING FOX, running well on a new diagram involving the 12.20pm 'Northumbrian' from King's Cross, which was taken from Grantham to Newcastle. In four weeks this elderly engine ran just under 8,700 miles and would have done more but for loss of Sunday trains due to labour troubles.

Sadly Grantham's reward for all this dedication came with the summer timetable in June 1950 when the new British Railways regime decided that most East Coast through trains would not change engines between London and Leeds and London and Newcastle. Pacifics were transferred away from Grantham except for two A3s and two A4s covering four diagrams of which only the 8.24am 'Mark Lane' went to King's Cross. The men continued,

NOCTURNE is a favourite feature from the pages of our parent magazine, *British Railways Illustrated;* perhaps the best known practitioners of this individual nocturnal art is G.F. HEIRON whose work (unbeknownst to him) published in such as *Trains Illustrated* many years ago, inspired this feature in the first place. So, it is a great pleasure to bring three examples to these pages now. At time of writing, the sun blazes and hosepipe bans threaten. Hopefully the usual seasonal fogs and chill will envelope you, the reader, as you come upon these pages - for the steam locomotive at night is somehow ineluctably associated with *cold.*

Left. A frosty night and Britannia Pacific 70016 *ARIEL* is enveloped in steam during a pause at Badminton station, with the 2pm Neyland - Paddington Sundays only express.

Above. With an unreal gleam, washed in the station lights, 6007 *KING WILLIAM III* pauses at Bristol Temple Meads, Platform 5, with the 4.15pm Paddington - Plymouth express, January 1958.

Below. Surreal, Black Five No.44855 grinds to a halt with an express from Birmingham at Temple Meads, in the early 1950s.
All three photos G.F. Heiron.

WAR REPORT

Perhaps the biggest gap in the vast photographic archive (in both public and private hands) is that due to the Second World War. There were many reasons. Real fears existed that a Fifth Column might be at work and anyone holding up a camera, particularly in the sensitive invasion-prone south, was liable to instant arrest and some rough handling - maybe prison. Many photographers were soon in one of the services, with little opportunity for camera work and film, moreover, became instantly scarce - an 'under the counter' item at best. Though much 'official' material has survived, faithfully recording bomb and rocket damage, or serving as propaganda to keep up home spirits, of the everyday train, in its ordinary environment in the years 1939-1945, there is very little indeed. So, we're grateful to *Reg Batten's* activities, overcoming problems of opportunity and lack of materials.

SAPPER WITH A CAMERA - MEMORIES IN WARTIME

Before the war I had been a keen photographer of railways and the countryside, travelling throughout the Home Counties and East Anglia by bike or train with my camera ever at hand. Upon the outbreak of war it looked as if my activities would have to be suspended; photography was discouraged or restricted, being viewed with suspicion as possible spying. As the war progressed, moreover, leisure travel was to be actively discouraged, the railways being hard-pressed to meet the wartime demands. *Is your journey really necessary?* exhorted that well known wartime poster - it has been much reproduced in recent years, to become something of a period icon, but

there was a reality behind it; it was enforced as far as possible, and travel became increasingly difficult.

A compositor in the printing trade, I was classified as being in a 'restricted' occupation at first and so not conscripted, but the rules were changed and I received my call-up papers in 1941. I entered the Royal Engineers as a draughtsman and photographer. This was somewhat ironic for me, as I had earlier applied for a post of draughtsman with the LNER at Stratford Works, only to be turned down on medical grounds.

I soon discovered that there is a silver lining to every cloud and army life was to open several new opportunities

to pursue my interests. For one thing my postings to various locations meant I could travel on strange lines and behind unfamiliar locomotive classes - opportunities otherwise probably denied to me, if only for want of the money to do so. Thus, an armourers' course in the Ordnance Depot at Burscough in Lancashire gave me a chance to ride behind the excellent L&YR Aspinall 2-4-2 radial tanks on the line into Ormskirk. I did not attempt to keep records of any of my journeys or the loco numbers involved - any such notes might have been viewed with deep suspicion if found by the military police! One particular locomotive I can never forget was Gresley A4 No.4469 SIR RALPH WEDGWOOD, originally GADWALL. This came on in the course of a journey to Guide Bridge and in hindsight I consider myself highly fortunate to have been behind it, for this was the unfortunate victim destroyed in an air raid at York station in April 1942, along with B16 No.925. The nameplates survived and were later transferred to No.4466 HERRING GULL.

I also found ways to continue my photographic exploits. I was given the job of Unit Armourer, for which I had

Unidentified Castle 4-6-0 on a down stopping train to Gobowen crosses Chirk viaduct; the aqueduct carrying the Shropshire Grand Union Canal is in the foreground. July 1944. Photograph R.E. Batten.

a comprehensive set of tools. I took full advantage of this and kept a camera at the bottom of the green-baize lined toolbox. The key to this was kept in the guardroom and except for the RSM I had sole access. When off duty, I could collect my camera and carry it in a pocket of the battledress intended for a first aid kit. Although railway photography was not banned as such, the taking of war related activities was prohibited. With the railways playing a crucial role moving troops and munitions, they were regarded as of strategic importance so in practice any production of a camera or even a notebook was likely to be challenged by the authorities.

Although I was in military uniform this did not entitle me to be on the line or exempt me from any restrictions on photography. Consequently I did not attempt to use my camera in London or other cities, generally keeping to remote rural areas. Luckily favourite peacetime locations around Potters Bar and Elstree were sufficiently secluded to be of use when I was on home leave. I never had any problems from loco crews or track and signalling staff - the latter probably thought I was there to guard the railway. Indeed I had more trouble photographing farmhouses, churches and so on. On one occasion whilst on leave and in 'civvies' I was arrested near Cheshunt while photographing buildings. Not satisfied with my explanations the police took me before the local army commandant. When ordered to produce ID I presented my AB64 army papers and claimed I was on intelligence business - whereupon I was released and invited

to take a meal in the camp canteen!

I spent three and a half years of the war based at Ruabon. During this time I had many happy hours of free time on the lines between Barmouth and Ruabon via Llangollen (part of which survives as the preserved Llangollen Railway) as well as on the main Shrewsbury to Chester line around Wrexham and Gobowen. A wide variety of GWR types could be seen and heavy freight trains were common. There were local stopping trains for miners at the then thriving collieries around Wrexham - antiquated clerestory roofed coaches hauled by 14XX 0-4-2Ts. Photographic trips were not always successful. One particular foray I recall was a disaster from start to finish, for a number of bizarre reasons. Whilst stationed at Ripon I decided, one free Saturday, to visit the lovely old town of Knaresborough. There is a charming view of the town with the railway bridge over the river Nidd in the foreground and the church in the background, a view I had sometimes seen in *The Railway Magazine* and wished to try for myself. As a lifelong Gresley fan, I also wished to take the D49 'Hunts' and 'Shires' that operated in the area. I boarded the bus at Ripon, and all seemed well until the vehicle suddenly lurched to one side, skirted a ditch and ended up in a field. There were no injuries but we were kept waiting till a relief bus arrived to take us onwards. Armed with military initiative, I had started walking over the fields towards the river and railway bridge, only to be apprehended by several soldiers of another corps, Royal Signals, and taken under escort be-

0-4-2T No.4811 hurries a miners' special down the line near Ruabon, August 1945. Photograph R.E. Batten.

Hall 4-6-0 on a down goods near Ruabon, August 1945. Photograph R.E. Batten.

fore their commanding officer. They were engaged on an exercise and as a member of a different unit (RE) and out of bounds in their area, I was, *de facto*, an 'enemy'. I was taken 'prisoner' and although well fed was held until 4pm. By then the light was unsuitable for photography so I went to the cinema before returning to Ripon for lights out.

Wartime traffic grew increasingly heavy. The varying fortunes in the field brought varying pressures on the railways and tested the ingenuity of the traffic controllers to meet all the demands. At the outbreak of war there had been the mass evacuation of chil-dren. Troop and munitions trains ran as required. Secondary through routes such as the Severn Valley line were used to relieve pressure on the main lines. Even so, freight trains could be held for hours in loops and sidings waiting for a path. Restaurant and sleeping car facilities were reduced or

LNER B17 4-6-0 No.1629 NAWORTH CASTLE leaving Norwich Thorpe station with an up express to Liverpool Street, September 1943. Photograph R.E. Batten.

Black 5 No.5191 passing Bourne End on a down train, in the month of Normandy, June 1944. Photograph R.E. Batten.

withdrawn on many routes. Locomotive stock was hard stretched and many engines due for replacement were given a reprieve. Some relief for the railway companies came when Stanier 2-8-0s, built initially as a War Department standard, were put into service. American built 2-8-0s followed in 1942 and the Riddles WD 2-8-0s and 2-10-0s first appeared in 1943. The deployment of these classes has been well documented elsewhere. Liveries were simplified in order to reduce costs, even GWR locos (except for 'Castles' and 'Kings') receiving unlined black livery on repaint. Standards of cleaning inevitably fell, making identification of engines in some photos impossible.

An interesting situation came about from 1944 whereby LNER B12 4-6-0s

K3 Mogul garbed in wartime grime, leaving the north end of the tunnel at Potters Bar, August 1944. Photograph R.E. Batten.

were used to haul ambulance trains throughout the country. They were chosen because of their low axle load 'go-anywhere' capability, the trains working as a fixed formation with the engine crew and other staff staying with the train throughout. Local pilots were taken and often local pilot engines.

The railways suffered heavily from bombing. Major stations such as York, Kings Cross, Bristol Temple Meads and St. Pancras were hit - the first two, and others indeed, have been documented in the pages of BRILL. Marshalling yards, works and docks were strategic targets. My home was at Canning Town in the heart of London's East End dockland (again detailed in the regular *War Reports* in BRILL) so my local line from Stratford to North Woolwich was in the front line of the London bombing raids. North Woolwich station lost its original ridged roof and was later rebuilt with the flat roof it retains now, in its role as museum. A flying bomb destroyed a railway bridge at Grove End Road, Bow on 13th June 1944 and in 1943 the engine of a Liverpool Street - Harwich train fell into a

crater near Ingatestone. Sadly the driver and fireman were killed in this incident, just two amongst many wartime railway fatalities.

One day in 1941 while returning on leave from Ripon I happened to see Sir Nigel Gresley crossing the footbridge on Kings Cross station. I noticed then how tired and worn he looked; a few weeks later I heard that he had died.

Life in the RE's often brought us into contact with railway operations. One posting I had was to Ashford, Kent at the Area No.1 Command Workshops. We used to use the baths at the railway workshops, and here (the shops not the baths) I was to get my first sight of the unusually-styled Bulleid Q1 0-6-0s, for Nos. C17-20 were built at Ashford. I did not see any of the Pacifics here though, for the Merchant Navies did not work on the Eastern division before 1944 and the West Counties were yet to appear. Ashford works was hit on a number of occasions by enemy bombers and we had several callouts to replace bridges damaged in air raids or by flooding. We built Bailey bridges, across the Medway for instance, after raids on the Maidstone

area. I was also working on drawings of mobile workshop trucks with expandable body sides, designed for General Montgomery's desert campaign against Rommel. Our commandant, Colonel Collingwood, was a director of Vulcan Foundry in peacetime.

Later I was based at Ripon where I met the artist Terence Cuneo. We were in the survey department processing 5in x 5in aerial photographs for the RAF. Our unit also had to blow up several bridges and viaducts and photograph the process. This was a dangerous job done in full battle gear and steel helmet. From there I was posted to Ruabon, where we were often called out in the middle of the night to deal with landslips on the section where the railway, river and Holyhead road ran in parallel. The Royal Engineers supplied the expertise and the Pioneer Corps supplied the muscle for these operations. On the night of 6th September 1945 the Shropshire Union Canal burst its banks between Llangollen and Ruabon, washing away the earthworks of the railway and leaving the track suspended in the air. GWR 2-6-0 No.6315 working a goods

WD 2-8-0 on down heavy freight near Brookmans Park, 1944. Photograph R.E. Batten.

and mail train arrived before the damage was discovered and plunged down the bank. We were called out to help make matters good but neither we nor the GWR could do anything to lift the loco, which was cut up on site. We were also called out to help with fires at the Monsanto chemical works at Cefn Mawr.

On an earlier occasion, with 250 Field Co. in Norfolk, we were being given a demonstration of setting explosives with gun cotton primers and a ring main circuit. Our unit was located alongside the LNER Norwich - Yarmouth line at Brundall Gardens. The officer in charge picked on me, declaring that I had not been paying attention to what he had been explaining (I did have one eye on the railway!) and told me to demonstrate before the whole platoon what he had been talking about. I did exactly that, placing the primers in contact with the exploders and intoning that "you gently press the exploder lever down and finally give it a jerk..." accompanying my words with the appropriate actions. The explosive charge detonated with an almighty bang, causing extensive damage to the adjacent level crossing. The officer hadn't intended for the explosives to be set off for real but was to late to stop me. He judged me responsible and I was put on a charge and later 'admonished'.

For the would-be wartime photographer legal restrictions were not the only limiting factor - there was the problem of obtaining the necessary film and other equipment. It could not be bought openly. I could only obtain 120 size film on home leave from my friends at Kodak in Kingsway who kept some 'under the counter' or at other shops

SR Paddlebox 4-6-0 No.444 on a down special of Army vehicles, passing West Byfleet in September 1944. Photograph R.E. Batten.

in the London area where I was 'known'. 35mm film was easier to get and I converted a camera from 16 to 120 on 35mm making the suitable masks and mechanisms.

Another idea was to make wooden templates for cutting up lengths of film used by the RAF, attaching it to the backing paper of used 120 film, then respooling it. This film was not really suitable for general use, being too fast and 'contrasty', but the spivs cottoned on and such film was sold on the black market. The most unscrupulous sold stuff which, on opening, turned out to have no film at all inside! Photographic chemicals were also in short supply. Paper was more readily available as the Americans brought their own and boxes of 5in x 5in paper were being sold on the black market. It was of poor quality, glossy both sides and difficult to glaze.

The Army darkroom at Ripon was in a Nissen hut, boiling hot in summer with little ventilation because of the blackout. It was the opposite of Ruabon where the stables were used on the Wynnstay estate where we were quartered. They had been dirty and cold and we made do with an old paraffin stove to keep the temperature up to 65/70F. Both aerial and circuit camera films of several feet in length were developed by a seesaw method, dipping it in large dishes on the floor.

Prior to the outbreak of war the Germans had built a factory at Biggleswade, making a film called 'Nuro'. This was of first class quality and I happily used a lot, obtaining some satisfactory results - the firm ceased production suddenly and I later heard that it had been a 'cover' for a spying operation. The story went that some directors were rounded up and imprisoned - or maybe hanged. The supply soon ran out but it was good while it lasted...

While the Germans turned out vast numbers of enhanced cameras to meet the needs of their armed forces, the British were unprepared in this respect. Leicas and Rollies were requisitioned by the government from photographic dealers and laws introduced forbidding the buying and exchanging of cameras. Daily notices were dispatched by the police to dealers, detailing stolen and missing cameras. Cameras brought into the country and offered for sale could be confiscated and the owners prosecuted.

VE Day came while I was still based at Ruabon. Correctly surmising that restrictions would not be enforced on this of all days, I decided to bunk the GWR loco shed at Oswestry. Several ex-Cambrian Railway locos were present and I photographed 2-4-0 LADY MARGARET. Later in the day we were entertained by the WVS and all food and drink was supplied free to the troops.

Shortly afterwards our whole unit was moved en masse to the ex-USA hospital at Longleat House near

Rebuilt Royal Scot No.6159 THE ROYAL AIR FORCE making a fair enough show of things despite the wartime neglect, at Bourne End, June 1944. Photograph R.E. Batten.

The official version of the war photograph had the incalculable advantage of suitable film, allied to access. This is Stewarts Lane shed yard, on 31st July 1944, and the damage to the great depository building would be the result of rocket attack. One of the *dis*advantages of 'official' railway photographs of course, is that locos and trains were regarded as things 'in the way of' a good photographic record, so they tend to be incidental to many of these Southern Railway images. This view is thus unusual in showing locomotives, a Southern 4-4-0 which looks to be out of action and, by an astonishing chance, a passing 'foreigner' in the shape of an LMS 4F 0-6-0.

Bomb damage at Wandsworth Common station, the day after, 24th September 1940. Attacks on railways, to be effective, had to be devastating and *sustained*, time after time. While a bombing episode such as this was destructive, and often tragic, what it brought about, essentially, was a mess, and a mess soon cleared up by the labour of men with shovels and a tank engine sent out with a few wagons to dispose of the rubble - often, most profitably, used for filling bomb craters further down the line...

Warminster. I was attached to the HQ staff and had no guard duties to interfere with my photography. In February 1946 I decided to visit the Somerset and Dorset but I heard that Charlton Road viaduct at Shepton Mallet, 317 yards long and of 27 arches had partially collapsed - so I thought it prudent to defer my visit. Shortly after I heard that I was to be demobbed and I never did get around to visiting the SDJR.

Demobilisation was to take place at Taunton. We were taken by truck to Warminster station to catch the train; when this came, to my surprise it was one of the GWR diesel railcars, a new experience for me. This stopped at all stations to Taunton, an interesting if somewhat tedious journey. After I had been fitted out with 'civvies' and taken a meal, I came back behind No.5013 ABERGAVENNY CASTLE first stop Westbury - which was more like it! I handed in my army gear and left for home and civvy street, back to London behind another Castle fast to Paddington with only a stop at Reading. My five and a half years of National Service done and many rolls of film the richer for it.

Fratton roundhouse, much knocked about, on the morning of 10th January 1941.

Below:- Blast damage at Maidstone West, again presumably a result of a rocket, on 3rd August 1944. Classic damage, with tiles lifted and windows gone (often blown *outwards*) but with the day to day of the railway untouched. Hand signalling would have been organised and a temporary cladding put on the building in no time. Though the combined resources of Bomber Command and the USAAF might have brought railways on the continent to a standstill, if they had been specifically directed to do so, the German air forces, despite bringing about endless disruption and mayhem, never *assaulted* Britain's railways as such, nor was there the wherewithal to carry out such a task. Nevertheless, great sorrow and loss came.

DIESEL DAWN
V SIGNS OF THE TIMES

Do not let it be thought that BR official diesel livery was simply decreed from above and imposed uniformly - there was some element of evolution at work... The BR 400hp 0-6-0 diesel shunter has been a familiar enough feature of Britain's railways for the best part of forty years, and there are twists and turns of detail and livery enough to delight the most masochistic amongst us. These two pictures of D3682 at Stratford on 7th September 1958, by an alert Alec Swain, show a hitherto unsuspected episode. Top - the V stripes, unusually, are seen to extend only half way up the cab but the bottom picture shows the stripes in more familiar disposition. Or are they? Closer inspection (I had to stare for some minutes before it dawned) reveals them to be *the wrong way up....*

LEICESTER'S MODERN ROUNDHOUSE

View looking south from close by the shed's traditional entrance in Beal Street. The Leicester engines became more and more confined, like fish in a drying pond, and the crowded yard beyond is largely obscured in smoke from the concentrated locomotives - the resuscitated roundhouse at Wigston served for much of the overflow. The cleared area immediately beyond the rising central 'ring' of the new roundhouse is the ground formerly occupied by the two original Leicester roundhouses, of ancient Midland lineage. Just discernible on the left is the three road straight shed, 'No.3 shed' and, betrayed by its whitewashed inner wall, the original stores and offices tacked onto the Midland buildings. Beyond that is the pitched roof of the old MR coaling shed.

By Ian Sixsmith

Though the subject was much debated over many years, especially in the post-war period, new engine shed building amounted really to renewal rather than wholly new building - though this could be very extensive indeed, reconstructing the shed from the ground up - witness the most effective exposition of this process, at Wakefield in the early 1950s, in BRILL 4.5. The process of renewal set in train on the LNER and LMS and to an extent the Southern continued after the war and under BR, but new work was concentrated very much on the rebuilding of existing sheds and the drive to mechanise coaling and ash disposal - a principal constraint being the availability of suitable sites. Urban sheds owed their usually nineteenth century) origins to and being available at the the-then edge of cities, and by the 1950s town growth had long surrounded them. There was not the money or more crucially the land, to move them further out - crews wouldn't wear it and in any case what of the stations and yards the sheds were built to serve? They could be moved even less readily, and BR found itself largely tied to its pre-grouping forms. The period of such work, moreover, was telescoped into a very few years, not getting underway properly till about 1947 and curtailed by the realisation that diesels and electrics were on the way.

Perhaps the most impressive of the 'renewal from the ground up' projects (Wakefield and others like it, remember, utilised the original nineteenth century ground plan, with its pits, drainage and suchlike) was the grandiose Leicester roundhouse and its associated yard and mechanical equipment. Leicester had been so bad, tumble-down and decrepit, that pre-war plans to rebuild were put into action as soon as could possibly be, immediately after war's end, but it was several years (another - probably unique - aspect) before the requisite and equally modern coal and ash plants were put up. Despite this, only at Leicester really, was the long story of shed development (got under way by the LMS) brought to a grand finale. At Upperby by contrast the modern equipment scheduled for the yard never materialised and at Crewe North, which was to have been the great crowning glory, cutbacks meant that the planned two great roundhouses were never built, only the marching rank of coal and ash towers and a cheaply built semi-roundhouse. Similar projects in the pipeline were curtailed, cut back, abandoned and cancelled and only at Thornaby was there

any comparable undertaking - and that was built with more than an eye on conversion to diesel working. At Leicester, with its later repair shop and coal and ash disposal plants, we have in effect the apogee of British engine shed development. In it is the coming together of all the threads of planning and development over the years; nowhere else did this thinking so materialise, in *all* its aspects.

By early 1952, however, before Leicester had received these mechanical aids to engine servicing, and it still struggled with an essentially Midland Railway yard layout, an official BR report had been confident of the way ahead; 36 depots had been analysed to provide the 'ideal shed' - 11 roundhouses (including Leicester?) with one, two three or four turntables and 22 straight sheds, either 'stump' as the report quaintly put it, or double ended. The three remaining depots examined comprised one fan type and two that were both roundhouse and straight sheds. Unfortunately they were not listed by name. To quote: *'advantages of a roundhouse type of shed are considerable; they provide greater protection from cold winds than straight sheds; the perimeter wall is continuous, except for the comparatively small archways for the incoming and outgoing roads, whereas the straight shed is* open for the entire width of the building, and in a through shed, at both ends.

'Locomotives may be stabled in any vacant berth, and once stabled there is no further movement required; work can be carried out upon the locomotive without interruption and in safety, and there is no shunting required to marshal the locomotives in order of departure times, as is necessary at straight sheds.

'The resulting saving in footplate staff is considerable, equal to 3.7 hours crew time per week per engine allocated; that is to say, at a straight shed having 50 engines allocated, four additional sets of footplate staff are employed upon shed duties compared with the roundhouse shed of similar allocation.'

The relative figures show differences in shunting and marshalling times - no less than 6.5 hours per week per engine for a straight shed and 2.8 hours per week per engine for a roundhouse. For a very few blithely untroubled years, new steam shed development, it was determined, would take this attractive roundhouse form, with highly mechanised yard. Within a year or so of Leicester coming fully into operation, however, diesels and electrics were established as *The Future*. There was little likelihood now of money for such developments, and apart from Thornaby, further steam shed construction came about almost as aberrations, such as Pwllheli and the Mexborough coaler, but that is another story...

Leicester shed nearing completion. View looking north. The works seem to have been carried out over the period 1945/6/7 (1947 is the date given in many of the photographs) and there is certainly some confusion as to the precise date of the work. The first proposals had come as early as the 1930s, for Leicester (apart from buildings at Derby long given over to other purposes) represented the last working Midland 'round' roundhouses, so tightly packed that cast iron inserts were made in the walls to take the buffers of engines! The buildings were ruinous even before the Second World War started and it is a measure of the severity of the conditions that the Chief Operating Manager issued a report actually in wartime, in 1940, as to its condition. Portions of the roofs had to be removed 'in the interests of safety' and a sum of £112,000 was approved for 'a new shed of octagonal shape with central turntable 70ft in diameter and 32 radiating roads' as well as mechanical plant, new tanks, new columns, electric light and so on. Work could not be got under way till war's end and from clearing the site to commissioning the coal/ash plants, it was thus spread over nearly ten years, from 1945 - 1954.

One of the sectors of the shed erected. The date of the photograph is given as 1947 though many accounts, including local reminiscence, give the completion of the shed as a year or so earlier - a measure of the post-war confusion. The progression of the works can be determined - first the turntable, then the laying down of some roads to provide the perfect device for delivering subsequent 'parts'. The LMS 'octagonal' shed gradually evolved, through a series of altered proposals and revisions, to the polygonal shape seen here. Upperby was similar and so were two roundhouses proposed for Crewe, but it is an historical afterthought that the octagonal shape was reverted to when Thornaby was built.

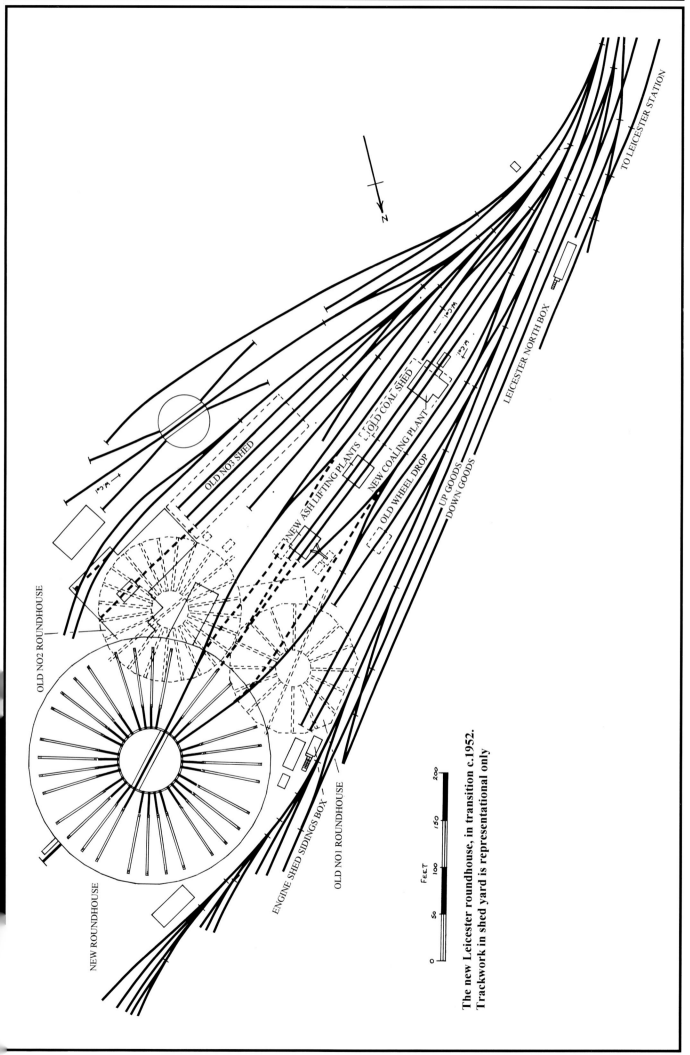

TO LEICESTER STATION

LEICESTER NORTH BOX

OLD NO3 SHED

NEW ASH LIFTING PLANTS

OLD COAL SHED

NEW COALING PLANT

OLD WHEEL DROP

UP GOODS

DOWN GOODS

OLD NO2 ROUNDHOUSE

NEW ROUNDHOUSE

ENGINE SHED SIDINGS BOX

OLD NO1 ROUNDHOUSE

FEET

0   50   100   150   200

**The new Leicester roundhouse, in transition c.1952.
Trackwork in shed yard is representational only**

Above:- Roof and shed well under way.
Below:- The new shed taking on its pleasing symmetry.

Above:- Inside the growing structure. Smoke troughs and uptakes had greatly exercised the engineers, technicians and scientists since well before the war, and there was a great growth in such studies immediately following 1945. On the LMS, particularly, it was felt that much of the high hopes of the vast new concrete building and re-roofing undertaken in the 'thirties had proved disappointing. The conventional 'square' roundhouses - those familiar high buildings of Midland, North Eastern and Great Western origin had, paradoxically, proved better for smoke removal than many of the modern buildings except, unfortunately, where the LMS had rebuilt them - at Belle Vue, Cricklewood and so on - in the new low style. Traditional roundhouse roofs were of high construction, 37/48ft to ridge and the chimney was clear of the ridge, providing a fair amount of draught almost directly above the locomotive's chimney and taking away smoke in a very satisfactory manner.

Below:- Close up of work on a particular sector, a perfect illustration of the almost 'kit building' nature of the job. Traditional pre-grouping roundhouses with their high pitched roofs leant themselves to the provision of independent smoke chutes, leading to single uptakes of chimneys, because locomotives were frequently berthed in a particular position. The Leicester smoke chutes were little different from the continuous troughs to be found at any number of straight sheds rebuilt in the period and BR was never to build the ideal high-roofed traditional type roundhouse - for reasons of expense. Leicester, however, never suffered any smoke problems and this was for two main reasons. The open middle acted like a vast chimney and allowed the breeze through at all times and secondly its dirtier, more actively smoke-generating denizens - that is, the 'turnback engines' that were simply serviced and sent out again after a short period - would be dealt with on the outside turntable which had been put in donkeys' years before by the Midland, as the old roundhouse sheds themselves became more and more unusable due to shortage of space. So, whilst Leicester shed was of tremendously modern aspect, its smoke removal relied upon traditional breeze, luck, weather and the rest - see, again, the scientific results of such investigations under Wakefield, BRILL 4.5.

Above:- Though all the engines present are 'tender outwards' there was no particular order to the putting away of engines in the new roundhouse; again this reflected the fact that 'turnback' engines were dealt with outside in the yard. Engines in the roundhouse proper were simply tucked wherever the next suitable road lay.

Below:- Clutter and debris outside the brand new shed. 2-8-0 No.8356 stands partly in the light.

Above:- New roundhouse, awaiting one or two final segments. The Crab 2-6-0 stands on one of a couple of truncated roads which formerly swept completely around the old Midland roundhouses to the far rear of the premises (now almost entirely occupied by the new shed). The little 3F 0-6-0, 3333, stands on one of the surviving roads of the (formerly 24 road) 'round' roundhouse, known as 'engine shed No.2'. The fragment of building close by the 0-6-0's tender was formerly attached to the outside of this easternmost of the Midland buildings.

Below:- Virtually complete and a menacing sky (or more probably a darkroom accident) giving an unreal, leaden quality to the place. In a dreary, rationed Britain, mired in an economic winter, the building was a startlingly modern one indeed.

The next phase of rebuilding at Leicester came in the early 'fifties and brought more piles of bricks, sand, pipes and all the rest. Almost the only feature of the Midland premises to be retained was the outside 60ft turntable, effectively giving Leicester two distinct areas of activity - 'home' engines or engines on prolonged diagrams which retired to the roundhouse and the quick 'turnback' locos which sat by the turntable or on the spurs provided off it.

September 1953 and the coaling plant and ash towers are well advanced at Leicester - they are entirely reminiscent of the arrangements at Crewe North. The overhead loading of ashes had been pioneered and developed on the LMS and existed almost nowhere else. As with so many motive power department ideas it was these LMS notions which were put into effect on BR though the ash towers, it seems, remained a London Midland specialism. It came as some surprise (as well as consternation) to BR officers in the early 'fifties that there was no real way to measure the efficiency of the various methods of ash disposal. Clearly wherever some mechanical or other method existed which obviated manual labour, ashes were cleared quicker but facts and figures were scarce. There had never been a call to record the amount of ash despatched from any shed for instance, and the total amount dealt with was a matter of estimation. To illustrate this point, on one Region six motive power depots used 6,000 tons of coal per week to make a notional 742 tons of ash whereas on another Region six depots used 9,200 tons of coal to make what was recorded as only 495 tons of ash... The cost per ton of loading ashes varied from 1/7d per ton to 8/6d per ton using skip hoists such as these and from 1/9d to 9/2d per ton for manual work. The wet ash pit at Darnall involved a cost of 2/6d per ton whilst that at Darlington 6/6d per ton... The professionals remained at a loss to explain these differences.

24th October 1959, the day of delivery for 0-6-0 shunters D3785, D3786, D3787 and D3788. Deep in the shadows of the surrounding houses, the old Midland turntable can just be discerned in the foreground. Photograph Les Wade.

Leicester shed, Sunday 2nd May 1965 with right, Jubilee 44573 NEWFOUNDLAND and left, 8F 48699. There was to have been a new 75,000 gallon water tank though the earlier structure shown here was retained. A major feature of the early 1950s work was the machine shop, the modern building set to the left. These engines are standing on the 'turnback' spurs, largely the same as the old Midland roads. Photograph H.A. Gamble.

8F No.48698 sits quietly at the rear of the shed with dome cover removed, Sunday 6th June 1965. Photograph H.A. Gamble.

Above:- The fine side view of Stanier Mogul 42955 is slightly marred by the wires running across but this is a wonderful depiction of the perennial crowding in Leicester shed yard. Oh, to be back there now! The possession of a fine new separate machine shop gave the shed a slightly eccentric place in motive power matters in the district. The concentration, or A shed, was for long Wellingborough but Leicester, far better equipped than most 'garage' sheds, was expected to do its own repair work (it acquired Wellingborough's 15A code in 1963). It also did much of the valve and piston work for Coalville which was under Leicester's wing rather than Wellingborough's and by at least 1959 it was also expected to do work for the other shed in the city, the physically remote ex-GC Central. The ex-GN Belgrave Road shed closed in 1956. Parts and fitters careered around the city in a van, for the places were far apart by rail yet close enough to have postal deliveries mixed up. The roundhouse had to be specified as 'Beal Street' to distinguish it from its GC neighbour. Photograph H.A. Gamble.

Below:- Jubilee 45585 on 3rd March 1961. It had been stuck with a cracked frame and on this day, the usual 3F tank being unavailable, was put on the loco yard pilot job, much to the discomfiture of the (appalled) regular crew. Photograph Alec Swain.

Above:- 12th August 1960 and Standard 4-6-0 No.75023, of Gloucester Barnwood of all places and in lined green livery to boot, makes a fuss of the turntable. The shed was really *too* well ventilated for winter work or delicate operations and side screens over certain bays were put up with sliding doors at the front, so that valve and piston exams could be quietly and, more importantly, cleanly carried out. Photograph Alec Swain.

Below:- Leicester, 3rd March 1961 with 0-6-0 No.44020 off a Wellingborough - Leicester passenger turn. The engine stands under the goods coal chute. Photograph Alec Swain.

Above:- Ivatt 4MT No.43022 on 'turnback' (its shedplate reveals it to be a Nuneaton engine) on 27th June 1960. Photograph Alec Swain.

Below:- 2nd March 1961, with Patriot 45537 PRIVATE E. SYKES VC on the outside turntable. To the left is the modern machine block, a feature almost unheard of at the great majority of sheds - it heralded the way forward in 1952/53. The sound of diesels over the horizon meant such buildings were not promulgated elsewhere. Its approach occupied the three roads of the old Midland straight shed ('shed No.3') but this new building was put up further back, a steel-framed structure which abutted on to the roundhouse behind and was connected internally therewith. It had only a single road and therefore plenty of room for machinery and stores; the canopy on the side in fact (another undreamt-of luxury) was for unloading wagons of spare parts directly into the stores area. The single road of the building served the wheeldrop - engines would be shunted in tender first, the relevant wheel sets taken out and the engine removed to stand in the yard until its wheels were ready. The wheeldrop was also the easiest method of changing springs, so it was more or less in constant use. There was sufficient space inside at the end of the single repair road to hold a diesel shunter and here, close by the mechanical foreman's office, all the 350hp diesel exams were carried out, independent of the incoming and outgoing procession of steam locos. Photograph Alec Swain.

Above:- D80 on driver training at Leicester, 3rd March 1961. Photograph Alec Swain.

Below:- 8F No.48221 in the 'turnback' part of the yard, 25th March 1961. Photograph A. Swain.

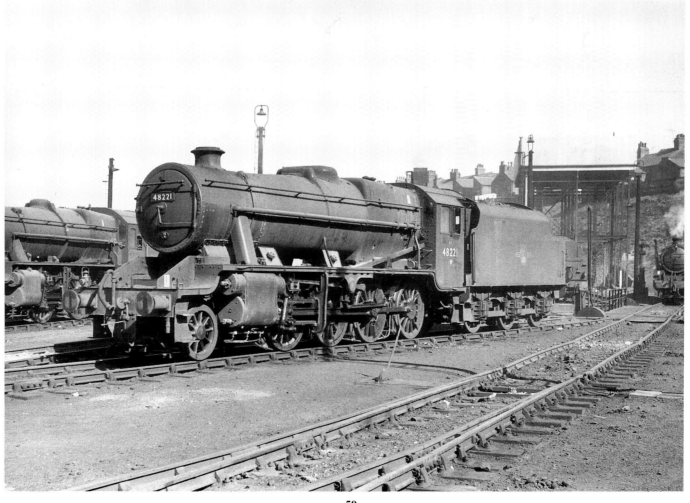

Above:- V2 2-6-2 No.60890 prepares to leave light engine for Leicester GC shed, after repairs - crewed by Toton men! Photograph A. Swain.

Below:- B16 4-6-0 No.61440 on one of the 'turnback' roads, 12th July 1960. The B16 is in course of a journey light engine to Darlington works - running as a 4-4-2! The rear side rods are lashed to the running plate with a rope around the leading splasher, in traditional fashion. Photograph A. Swain.

Above:- 2nd May 1965. By this time much of the home complement had been done away with and the shed reduced, in terms of steam, more and more to the status of a servicing point - thus the preponderance of diesels in the yard. Locos are 78027, 45573 NEWFOUNDLAND, 48699 and D70 THE ROYAL MARINES. Photograph Locofotos.

Below:- The 'turnback' corner on 8th August 1965, with 41212, 48637 and 90227. This unique steam shed closed in June 1966 and though it housed the preserved MR locos for a while, was demolished in the 1970s. Photograph Locofotos.

This was the hard way to move the milk although this gang of porters at Kensington Addison Road circa 1935 seem cheerful enough. C.R.L.Coles.

ON THE MILK

This is a story of the rise and eventual decline of milk traffic, once so common on our railways. Milk was carried, in one simple form or another, from the earliest days and was to remain a regular business until the early 1980s when finally, along with so many other traffics, the last of went to road. How did it all start and why and how did it all finish? Beginnings lie back in the nineteenth century, when the industrial revolution was in full swing and the railway was increasingly coming into its own, serving the growing needs of the nation.

From the 1840s milk had gone by train. Parts of London received milk from Essex to supplement locally produced supplies but the expansion of the population in general and the capital in particular during the latter half of the nineteenth century, along with an outbreak of cattle disease in the London herds, meant that milk was required from farther afield. The railways had the means to get the milk from producing areas hundreds of miles away, in a condition still fresh enough for consumption. Specially constructed vans were dedicated for the milk, each of them holding dozens of churns. Rainfall means that the main milk producing areas of Britain are on the western side of the country, the wetter weather producing a more lush grass. There were a number of districts given over to milk in East Anglia but dry summers could cut production drastically, sometimes to the point where milk was imported from the West Country.

Surviving records of Great Western milk traffic sent to London during specific periods gives us a good idea of the

growth and needs of the capital during the latter period of the nineteenth century. And remember, this was but one of the companies serving London.

The Great Western was probably responsible for the first ever transport of milk by train and fittingly enough, after nearly a century and a half of lucrative business, the Western Region ran the last regular services, from Cornwall, Devon and west Wales. Clas-

MILK RECEIVED AT PADDINGTON 1869-1870				
Week	Gallons	Cans	Gallons	Cans
1	33,240	2,295	39,941	2,702
2	35,046	2,469	37,941	2,634
3	36,579	2,538	36,041	2,558
4	34,408	2,413	36,571	2,574
total	139,273	9715	150,494	10,468

MILK RECEIVED AT PADDINGTON, JAN.1884		
From	Gallons	Cans
Bleadon	265	16
Bridgwater	755	55
Castle Cary	8,826	660
Devizes	22,792	1,575
Evesham	14	1
Faringdon	24,401	1,813
Oxford	1,009	162
Quainton Road	3,649	293
Swindon	28,707	2,107
Verney Junction	86	7
Witney	3,098	258

Altogether 527,293 gallons were received by Padington during this period in 39,684 cans. A few of the representative stations and their outputs are given above.

Paddington, and churns stand round about; a familiar enough platform accessory across the country.

Left:- Enter the milk tank. This is one of the new GWR glass lined, 3,000 gallon tanks positioned for loading at the purpose built Wootton Bassett, Wiltshire, depot of United Dairies. The valve at the bottom of the tank is the discharge valve which, once secured, was padlocked until arrival for unloading at Mitre Bridge, London. All the tanks subsequently built were piped for vacuum and steam heating when running in passenger trains. The tank in view is No.2010. Michael.C.Shaw collection.

Below:_ Top view of 2010 being loaded at Wootton Bassett. The various tank fittings, from left to right, are the safety valve, compressed air inlet, man-hole, filler valve. The funnel was part of the dairy equipment and was removed when filling was complete. At the receiving depot the tanks were washed out after unloading, rinsed twice, steam sterilised and sealed for return. Hygiene was of the utmost importance and the boast was that during the whole process milk was untouched by any outside element after it had arrived from the farm. Michael.C.Shaw collection.

sified as passenger rolling stock by all the railway companies, the milk carrying vehicles of the Great Western, some 1,450 various items of stock, accounted for 14% of its total passenger vehicle fleet in 1924. Similar proportions could be found on the other companies - the London & South Western Railway for instance, had been send-ing three milk trains a day to London before the Great War, from Dorset and Somerset, and this was naturally continued under the Southern.

Provincial cities relied in the main on locally produced milk from herds grazing in the surrounding country, though the railways meant it could be supplemented from districts further off

- Manchester's milk for example, came in large part from the Fylde, some fifty miles away, the Lancashire & Yorkshire Railway doing the honours on a daily basis in dedicated vans. For a long period during World War Two and its aftermath, Liverpool received a daily train of milk from North Wales, originating in Bangor.

GLASS LINED

Four of the GWR/United Dairies fleet on the milk depot spur at Wootton Bassett in November 1927. The Great Western milk tank fleet, including those built in the early BR period, eventually numbered more than 350 vehicles. Michael.C.Shaw collection.

Milk, as with almost any account of railways in this country, is one of decline:

Study of the two tables 1923/24 and 1933/34 shows a definite trend downwards in the carriage of milk and a fall in receipts during the mid-1930s compared with the previous decade. By April 1939 this trend was continuing, with gross receipts down to £72,000 for just under thirteen and a half million gallons carried that month. Competition from road carriers was biting. Nearly half of the total milk traffic conveyed by the railways had disappeared since 1919.

ENTER THE TANK

All of the Big Four companies and many of their constituents had a hand in the milk traffic. Over 280 million gallons of milk a year was transported by rail in the late 1920s and of this the LMS accounted for 95 million gallons whilst the GWR carried 85 million. It was pointed out in the railway press in 1927 that a train some *2,333 miles* long would be required to haul this annual amount if carried in churns, yet in the new 'tank' method a train only 689 miles long would suffice. Savings in time and manpower were there to be made in an age when the railways were hardly well-off for cash, and besides, road transport was already using 'tankers', having taken the initiative early on. In doing so, ominously, it was taking an ever larger bite into the milk market.

An example of the handling required with milk churns can be gained from

GALLONS MOVED AND RECEIPTS ACCRUED NATIONALLY 1923/24

Month	G.W.R.	L.N.E.R.	L.M.S.	S.R.	Total (galls)	Receipts (£)
Jun 1923	6,121,375	4,131,938	8,838,821	4,003,460	24,588,584	142,331
Jul 1923	6,550,197	4,046,203	9,442,100	3,968,153	25,678,098	152,707
Aug 1923	6,088,994	3,799,530	8,920,652	3,724,776	24,142,699	144,600
Sep 1923	6,287,389	3,511,834	8,759,541	3,425,838	23,361,415	140,611
Oct 1923	6,723,088	3,583,736	8,695,036	3,367,555	23,705,772	142,136
Nov 1923	6,503,166	3,489,450	8,335,863	3,362,814	23,030,465	138,527
Dec 1923	6,334,022	3,630,358	8,221,360	3,478,174	22,822,104	135,996
Jan 1924	6,209,141	3,507,957	8,345,741	3,384,887	22.454,286	132,565
Feb 1924	6,105,728	3,535,375	7,923,862	3,370,757	21,976,558	131,112
Mar 1924	6,523,536	3,863,345	8,702,259	3,696,345	23,897,088	142,840
Apr 1924	6,887,991	4,091,699	8,716,646	4,006,062	24,769,615	145,506
May 1924	6,547,098	4,012,609	8,681,992	3,848,607	24,162,520	141,835

GALLONS MOVED AND RECEIPTS ACCRUED NATIONALLY 1933/34

Month	G.W.R.	L.N.E.R.	L.M.S.	S.R.	Total (galls)	Receipts (£)
Jun 1933	4,966,342	2,739,033	5,740,113	2,275,359	16,247,497	92,498
Jul 1933	5,576,984	2,580,799	6,119,891	2,626,627	17,477,359	98,811
Aug 1933	5,291,972	2,355,181	6,127,836	2,611,536	17,098,661	99,668
Sep 1933	5,735,763	2,036,516	6,192,320	2,460,510	17,265,191	100,116
Oct 1933	5,095,478	2,000,013	5,803,719	2,379,419	15,894,024	89,060
Nov 1933	4,528,179	1,952,976	5,476,680	2,192,072	14,838,612	81,847
Dec 1933	4,605,226	2,097,494	5,411,686	2,203,582	15,078,845	83,401
Jan 1934	4,542,141	2,218,877	5,182,856	2,186,702	14,877,306	81,426
Feb 1934	3,937,644	2,038,637	5,069,170	1,937,569	13,648,002	76,023
Mar 1934	4,483,690	2,396,878	5,747,966	2,198,246	15,555,854	86,863
Apr 1934	4,462,596	2,322,931	4,866,973	2,134,269	14,355,176	79,233
May 1934	4,355,622	2,451,131	5,558,628	2,568,143	15,327,036	82,881

Close-up of one of the 4-wheel GW/UD tanks in 1927. After a number of derailments with the 4-wheel tanks a 6-wheel version was introduced which became standard throughout the industry. Early vehicles such as 2007 were converted to 6-wheelers. Michael.C.Shaw collection.

this abridged account of an article which appeared in the *Southern Railway Magazine*, late in 1927. "In the twelve months ended June 1927, the Southern Railway transported to London the equivalent of 1,469,312 full churns of milk. The numbers of churns received at the respective stations was:- Waterloo 139,850; Vauxhall 568,346; Clapham Junction 747,737; London Bridge 7,760; Victoria 5,152; Cannon Street 360; and Charing Cross 107. Each milk churn weighed approximately 56 pounds and contained 17 imperial gallons weighing 170 pounds. The bulk of the consignments were carried in four-wheeled vans accommodating 60 churns or about 6 tons and the vans tared at 12 tons each. The majority were marshalled and hauled in special trains; some however, were attached to ordinary passenger trains. It must be remembered that all of these churns and vans had to be returned empty to the districts and stations whence they came. For approximate calculation we will take just one million churns from that monthly total, which weigh empty some 25,000 tons, or 50,000 tons when their return is considered, to convey 75,890 tons of milk. Some 16,280 vans will be required, weighing 201,840 tons, and as these

One of the LMS/United Dairies tanks. This is No.638 in July 1928 after some nine months in service. Inspection of the freshly painted solebar reveals that the wagon was turned out from Derby on the 23rd November 1927 and the load was not to exceed 14 tons (3,000 gallons). The tank is already showing signs of in-service grime and as the years went by the tanks never seemed to be cleaned on the outside. The early LMS tanks built up to the 1932 received random and scattered numbers but by 1933 all were renumbered into a block in the 44XXX range. The large LMS fleet was further boosted by additions during the BR period and eventually numbered some 230 vehicles. Michael.C.Shaw collection.

Above and below:- Southern 4419 was built in 1932 for UD and was part of a second batch of 6-wheel tanks introduced in that year. Like the earlier tanks they too contained 3,000 gallons. 4419 was another vehicle which survived until the 1970s. J.Tatchell collection.

have to return also, no less than 403,680 tons of van tare-weight has to be hauled to perform this service. Add the weight of the empty churns and the total goes up to 453,680 tons of deadweight to be moved over each mile

to transport 75,890 tons of milk over the same distance. Now if all this was moved in tanks, and without bombarding the reader with further facts at this stage, the deadweight would drop by nearly two-thirds."

The case for tank transportation was unanswerable. Note was taken by all concerned and the flood gates were opened for the future bulk transport of milk. Over the next ten years the cost of milk transport was cut consid-

Most of the SR road trailer traffic was loaded at Salisbury and Gillingham (Dorset). This July 1939 view of Salisbury milk dock shows one of the Dyson UD 2,000 gallon trailer tanks (UD fleet No.T4) being secured for its journey to London. Churns are in evidence on the platform behind the road tractor and behind that are two Van U, 4-wheel utility vans, part of the large SR fleet extensively employed on churn traffic. J.Tatchell collection.

erably by the introduction of the railborne milk tank.

The first purpose-built rail tanks designed for the conveyance of milk were brought into service on 1st December 1927 by the United Dairies Ltd. in conjunction with the Great Western and the London Midland & Scottish Railways. The inaugural GWR service left a purpose-built depot at Wootton Bassett whilst the LMS train left from a similar plant at Calveley in Chesh-

ire. Both were bound for the United Dairies depot at Mitre Bridge (Willesden) where a reception committee ranging from railway company officials to representatives from the Ministries of Agriculture and Health, as well as various dairy organisations, inspected the unloading facility and the UD plant. Hygiene was the order of the day and the bulk transport of the milk meant less handling and therefore less chance of contamination. The insu-

lated, glass lined tanks had a capacity of 3,000 gallons, equal to more than 200 of the 10 and 17 gallon churns they replaced. At Mitre Bridge an existing siding connected to the United Dairies Scrubs Lane bottling depot and milk was unloaded from the rail tanks at the rate of 150 gallons a minute, using compressed air. This particular pasteurising and bottling plant boasted, at that time, the largest daily output of any such plant in the world

Two empty UD Dyson trailers waiting to be unloaded at Salisbury in 1934. Each trailer was fitted with a towing bar at each end enabling greater flexibility of movement. Michael.C.Shaw collection.

SR tank flat No.4414, one of seven 6-wheel flats operated by the Southern. All lasted until 1961 when mobile road tanker traffic was withdrawn. Three 4-wheel flats introduced by the SR in 1931 were not converted to 6-wheelers and last saw service in 1938. The Great western fleet consisted 34 of these vehicles, most of them dedicated to CWS traffic. J.Tatchell collection.

- no less than 46,000 gallons of milk a day left in bottles for retail sale.

On December 13th 1928 the LNER inaugurated a service employing seven new 3,000 gallon four wheeled tank wagons, on a nightly service from the former Great Northern station at Ingestre, Staffordshire to the United Dairies distribution depot at East Finchley on the High Barnet branch. Churns had previously been employed

for this service and the bulk transportation brought benefits not only from the hygienic glass lined tanks but also savings in labour-intensive handling. The churn was on its way out, though it would be nearly thirty years before it was eradicated completely.

A number of derailments occurred with the four-wheeled milk tanks shortly after they entered service. The 10 foot 6 inch wheelbase was not

suited to the travel at speed and consequently a new specification was brought in about 1930, which required that all future milk tanks would be either six-wheeled or have a 15 foot wheelbase, with no increase in capacity. The early four-wheeled vehicles were rebuilt to six-wheelers. The LNER *General Appendix* of 1937 stated that any passenger or milk train conveying 4-wheeled tanks must not exceed

Milk tank traffic workings were complicated but because of the nature of the product it was also very slick. This is Hemyock in Devon in late July 1958 with 0-4-2T No.1449 marshalling its train of full tanks from the dairy, just beyond the station, and pushing the empties into the establishment. After completion of that movement it would return to the station and collect the solitary passenger brake for the run to Tiverton Junction. R.C.Riley.

The Hemyock milk train approaches Tiverton Junction with 1449 in charge. At the junction the tanks will be attached to the 3.42 p.m. Exeter - Taunton from where they would join the 12.20 p.m. Penzance - Kensington milk train. R.C.Riley.

speeds of 60 miles per hour and 4-wheeled tanks must be marshalled with a six or eight-wheeled vehicle immediately behind them. By 1939 all the 4-wheel tanks had been converted. Milk trains were nevertheless involved in accidents - a Carmarthen - Paddington train consisting thirteen tanks and three Siphons derailed near Kidwelly in late 1945, resulting in a pile-up and 40,000 gallons of milk lost.

Tank wagon chassis were owned by the railway company and only the tank itself was the property of the named dairy. The tanks varied inasmuch as some were steel with fused glass lining, others were aluminium and lined and later examples were of stainless steel. Capacity in most cases was 3,000 gallons with some 2,000 gallon tanks and there were even a few with twin tanks (2,000/1,000 gallons) for

loading different grades of milk - Jersey or Fresian, say. All had one thing in common, in that they were insulated against the elements and it was stated that even on a hot summer's day the temperature of the milk in the tank would not rise more than two degrees throughout the journey. Of course the railway company moving the tanks, whether they were full or empty, treated them as urgent perishable traf-

4986 RYDAL HALL and 2-8-0 No.3832 on Dainton on 29th June 1957, with the 12.20pm Penzance - Kensington. R.C.Riley.

Uffculme, with 1450 shunting the day's 'milk'. David Lawrence.

fic - at least until the 1960s - but see later...

In the early part of 1931 another innovation came, from the Co-operative Wholesale Society and the Southern Railway, 4-wheel wagons specially built to carry 2,000 gallon road tank trailers with solid rubber road tyres, each trailer having six wheels. Pneumatic tyres were introduced two years later and this time the road trailers were reduced to four wheels, whereas the rail wagons to carry them were built as 6-wheelers. The road tankers were loaded onto the rail wagons which were specially constructed so that the weight (approx. 13 tons) of the tank and its load could be taken off the road tyres as the trailer was winched onto the wagon (see photographs for detail). Besides the CWS and Southern, the Great Western (in conjunction with United Dairies) introduced the new road-rail tanks shortly afterwards, followed by the LMS and certain of its customers. The Southern brought its handful into service working between Salisbury, Gillingham (Dorset) and the United Dairies depot at Forest Hill, London.

By the early 1930s about a dozen large dairy concerns had swallowed up most of the smaller independent pro-

Trip workings from the dairy to a junction or main line station was an everyday occurrence and trains varied in weight. This ex Wootton Bassett trip has just arrived at Swindon, in April 1964, behind pannier 9680 and will be forwarded to London on the next milk train from South Wales. The van, W117W, carries the legend WOOTTON BASSETT AND KENSINGTON MILK TRAIN and PARCELS TRAIN BRAKE VAN. A.Swain.

With a (in the circumstances incongruous) goat looking on, the solitary tank originating from the Garsdale branch (mentioned in the text) makes its way empty to the dairy behind J21 65038, along the branch past Finghall Lane in 1955. This tank was working a five hundred plus mile diagram each day, seven days a week - it was certainly utilised to the utmost. N.E.Stead collection.

ducers and of the big boys the following owned railtanks: Aplin & Barrett Ltd; Cow & Gate Ltd; CWS Ltd; Dried Milk Products Ltd; Express Dairies; Independent Milk Supply Co.; London Co-op; Mutual Dairies; Nestle, Anglo Swiss; United Dairies; West Park Dairy Co.

In an effort to co-ordinate the production and distribution of milk and generally to lift the milk producing industry out of depression, the Government created the Milk Marketing Board in 1933. The Milk Marketing Board guaranteed farmers a fixed price for milk and organised transport to the markets. Until recent times the MMB oversaw the running of the milk industry and it too had its own fleet of tanks, which were amongst the last to survive.

For an idea of the logistics involved in getting milk from the farm to the breakfast table, we can take a look at an arrangement set up in October 1932 between th Great Western and the Anglo-Swiss company Nestle, to transport the stuff from 600 Cornish farms to the two Nestle depots in London, at Battersea and Bow, every day.

The GWR provided the road transport and Nestle the churns for the round-the-clock collection of milk from nearly every farm in the county. Up to 7,000 gallons could be collected from each farm, though this was not the norm. A fleet of twenty-one lorries, ranging from 2 to 6 tons capacity, worked out of collection centres at Bodmin, Helston, Falmouth, Liskeard, Looe, Lostwithiel, Newquay, St Austell and Truro, each lorry making one or two journeys a day over the twenty-six collecting routes, depending on the size of route area covered. Empty churns were ex-

This up train approaching Rugby on the WCML in May 1939 comprises a milk flat with road trailer, a 2,000 gallon milk tank, two 3,000 gallon milk tanks and vans containing dairy products and churns, with a number of parcels vans behind. The locomotive is 5638 ZANZIBAR. Dairies the length and breadth of the Premier Line provided traffic for the LMS. Locofotos.

Penzance, July 1953 and the 6.20 p.m. Kensington milk train ready to leave for London behind 5023 BRECON CASTLE. Only the two tanks and the two vans constitute the milk train at this point; the train behind is the 6.40 p.m. Postal. At St Erth the milk train will 'go inside' to collect further tanks whilst the Postal passes. On its way the 6.20 will pick up more tanks originating off Cornish branches and will probably need a pilot to get over the South Devon banks. C.R.L.Coles.

changed at the farm for full 8-gallon capacity churns. Upon completion of its round the lorry, which could carry 50 churns, would return to its road-collection centre to unload them into railway vans for carriage to Lostwithiel, the Nestle receiving depot. In North Cornwall a six-ton lorry capable of conveying 135 churns was used to relieve one of the smaller two-ton road vehi-cles, enabling it to proceed to further farms in this remote area of the county. Once at the Lostwithiel receiving depot, the milk was tipped into a tank for weighing. It was then pumped into a storage tank from whence it flowed through cooling apparatus into the waiting rail tanks. The empty churns in the meantime were mechanically cleansed and dried ready for return to the farms. The rail tanks left Lostwithiel station daily by the 12.57 and 2.59 p.m. passenger trains for the 260 mile journey and an evening arrival in London. Besides the tanks there was also a small amount of churn traffic from Lostwithiel to Paddington and South Lambeth. Each Sunday saw a large consignment leave for a condensing factory at Trowbridge.

Another daily milk train originating in Cornwall, the 12.20 p.m. Penzance - Kensington, drifts through Menheniot behind 6801 AYLBURTON GRANGE in July 1956. R.C.Riley.

5958 KNOLTON HALL with down milk empties at Challow, 26th April 1959. R.C. Riley.

Magnify this enterprise to encompass all the milk producing areas of the kingdom and it is revealed as the vast undertaking it all was - it is easy to understand why the Milk Marketing Board was created.

SOME MILK TRAIN SERVICES

Documents to hand allow a more detailed look at some specific services - the **LNER North Eastern Area,** in common with its preceding NER archive material, is particularly well-represented in the Public Record Office at Kew, far beyond the detail available for many other railways and areas; it tells us that before 1900 Wensleydale milk travelled to London via both Great Northern and Midland routes. One particular working during the 1930s had one tank wagon a day, including Sunday, leaving Northallerton (1.08 pm weekdays) bound for Queens Park, London. This would be an LMS company tank wagon and its typical journey would be Northallerton - York - Leeds LMS - Queens Park; arrival at Leeds New was 2.46 pm. before onward transit to London. The Sunday working for this tank was a bit more interesting, there being no southbound working from Northallerton at the time the tank arrived off the Hawes branch - so it was sent north at 1.30 pm to Darlington where a slick turnround was required for its departure, attached to the 2.45 pm southbound express to York, where it arrived at 3.34 pm. Departure from York was at 4.00 pm for a 4.30 pm arrival in Leeds from where it departed south up the Midland main line at 5.08 pm. An av-

On 16th July 1958, and 4077 PEMBROKE CASTLE has charge of the 12.20 p.m. Penzance - Kensington milk as it rounds the bend at Cowley Bridge, Exeter. Sometimes this train could load up to 800 tons. R.C.Riley.

The Whitland milk empties snaking out of West Ealing, 31st July 1955. R.C.Riley.

erage 80,000 gallons a month were conveyed to Queens Park by this solitary tank. Over the period of the 1930s and 1940s this daily consignment caused the traffic department much consternation, for its late running off the Hawes branch could bring some operating problems. By 1949 the tank was travelling from Northallerton behind the 11.55 am Middlesbrough - Leeds passenger, departing Northallerton at 1.10 pm The cause of any late running lay usually with the farmers who, it must be said, were continually at loggerheads with the LNER, whose road vehicles collected

the milk from the farms. The tank would usually return empty up the branch in a mixed passenger/goods and at Leyburn a Sentinel (68159) would shunt the vehicle into a milk dock. Besides the solitary wagon destined for Queens Park there were milk vans coming off the branch heading for other destinations. Timings were tight to get the milk to the railheads, and complaints from all parties involved were an everyday occurrence. Not all the milk from Wensleydale was to end up on breakfast tables, for large quantities were purchased by the likes of chocolate manufacturers. In April

1954 the branch closed to passengers and the milk traffic - it was passenger rated remember - was lost to road.

Fluctuations in the amount of milk supplied at various periods would appear to be tremendous but there was

CONSIGNMENTS FROM THE HAWES BRANCH 1933/34			
Milk originating from the Hawes (Garsdale) area and received in London during the period Dec 1933 to Nov 1934 at the following points			
Month	Finsbury Park**	Kings Cross**	Queens Park*
Dec 1933	16,490	391	92,452
Jan 1934	14,535	5,933	89,311 (+3,689 churns)
Feb 1934	11,730	6,902	84,000
Mar 1934	9,690	6,902	93,139
Apr 1934	6,630	1,071	79,950
May 1934	2,040	7,600	75,155
Jun 1934	6,035	4,345	75,203
Jul 1934	2,240	4,650	57,178
Aug 1934	-	2,040	45,260
Sep 1934	-	-	24,280
Oct 1934	-	1,020	55,200
Nov 1934	-	1,020	35,900

* Cow & Gate dairy. All traffic in tanks.

** All traffic in cans

Once in London the re-working of milk trains became even more complicated than the workings on and off the branch lines whence the milk tanks originated. Tanks arriving from the LMS were tripped to dairies in south London and its outer suburbs. Some originating on the Southern would end up in east London, tripped via the GW, LMS and LNER lines. There was a mass of criss-crossing paths on a daily basis. This train of empties from the Express Dairy bottling plant at Morden South and bound for Willesden hauled by Class C 31690, passing Factory Junction, is a typical example of cross-London milk traffic. R.C.Riley.

usually an explanation. For instance in November 1934 milk traffic from the Hawes branch (Wensleydale) for onward transit via Northallerton amounted to 125,521 gallons but by the following November this was more than halved to 58,642 gallons. Alarm bells sounded in the Divisional offices and after investigation the Divisional General Manager was supplied with the explanation "that butter was now being manufactured in Northallerton and the equivalent of 71,280 gallons

Kensington became something of a marshalling point for milk traffic. Stewarts Lane Ivatt 2-6-2T No.41292 heads a train of five empty tanks from the SR to LMR, bound eventually for Dumfries, in August 1960. R.C.Riley.

of milk was converted to butter". During that November the LNER forwarded 251 hundredweight (12.52 tons) of butter by goods train from Northallerton and a further 392 pounds by passenger service. So all was well - for the time being.

On the **LNER GER Section** milk came daily in tanks from Halesworth in Suffolk for Ilford and London, as well as from the United Dairies creamery at North Elmham in Norfolk. Up to seven tanks a day would leave from the latter depot in the late afternoon, running via Norwich with the occa-sional van to carry other dairy products and churns. Road transport saw the North Elmham service finish at the end of 1963.

The LNER GN Section was important for milk too; by the late 1870s the Great Northern had built up a steady milk traffic from Lincolnshire and Staffordshire to the capital. The latter was the biggest milk producer area of the two counties and it was this traffic which the GN cultivated, to the point (by the turn of the century) when two trains were despatched each night. Milk from Northallerton traversed the main line to Finsbury Park and Kings Cross for onward movement to the outer suburbs. The introduction of bulk tanks saw the churn traffic drop considerably, the churns carrying Wensleydale milk ceasing in 1935.

THE TANK FLEET: SOME NOTE AND NUMBERS

What follows are outline notes only, with no claim to be definitive - the section on LNER vehicles for instance is merely a couple of specimen numbers. Doubtless a whole book could be written on the elucidation - design, con-

In among the allotments of west London, and pannier tank 9708 heads a train of empties from Kensington to West Ealing through Drayton Green in April 1955. R.C.Riley.

9708 arrives at West Ealing with its train of empties where, with empty tanks from other points, it will be made into a train for Whitland in west Wales. A number of tanks were unloaded into road tankers at West Ealing in a special bay constructed for the purpose. R.C.Riley.

struction and numbering, of these specialised vehicles. Any offers....?

GREAT WESTERN

GWR 4 wheel: 2001-2011, 2016, 2504, 2506,
2935 (6 wheel)twin tanks.
2960
No.1953, built 1944, 6-wheel UG
No.1955-57, Dia. 053 built 1944. 6-wheel CWS
No.1968-77, Dia. 054 built 1946. 6-wheel ED* (ex IMS)
Nos.1978-95, Dia. 055 built 1946. 6-wheel A&B
Nos.2009-16, Dia. 055 rebuilt 1932. 6-wheel.

Nos.2504-1, Dia. 055 built 1948-54. 6-wheel.
Nos.2512-17, Dia. 039 built 1934. 6-wheel UD
Nos.2531-36, Dia. 039 built 1934. 6-wheel UD
No.2557, Dia. 041 built 1935. 6-wheel ED twin tks.(ex-London CWS)
Nos.2561-63, Dia. 042 built 1935. 6-wheel ED*
Nos.2567-76, Dia. 042 built 1936. 6-wheel IMS
Nos.2587-92, Dia. 039 built 1936. 6-wheel UD
Nos.2593-94, Dia. 042 built 1935. 6-wheel ED*
Nos.2595-98, Dia. 042 built 1935. 6-

wheel ED*
No.2835, Dia. 042 built 1938. 6-wheel UG
No.2932, Dia. 042 6-wheel twin tanks.
No.2952, Dia. 042 built 1942. 6-wheel
No.2996, Dia. 042 built 1944. 6-wheel
Nos.3005-18, Dia. 042 built 1946. 6-wheel
Nos.3023-28, Dia. 058 built 1947. 6-wheel C&G
Nos.3029-35, Dia. 058 built 1946. 6-wheel
Nos.W3037-52, Dia. 058 built 1948.** 6-wheel
Nos.W3120-23, Dia. 058 built 1950.** 6-wheel C&G twin compartments 1 tank.

* Tanks numbered by Express Dairy. Some ED tanks had an extra cover over the top half of the tank.
** To GWR designs. All later (1950 onwards) BR vehicles were built to ex-GWR designs.
Abbreviations:
A&B = Aplin & Barrett Ltd.
C&G = Cow & Gate
CWS = Co-op Wholesale Society
ED = Express Dairy
IMS = Independent Milk Supplies
UD = United Dairy
UG = Unigate

GWR Milk Vans

Siphon G 1912-1927 various diagrams, outside frame (early) Siphon G, running numbers:- 1240-1269, 1271-1309, 1345-1364, 1442-1481.
Siphon G 1926-29 diagram 022, running numbers:- 1186-1200, 1223-1237, 1270.
Siphon G 1929-45 diagram 033, running numbers:- 2051-2070, 2751-

With its train now assembled, 4917 CROSSWOOD HALL leaves the milk dock at West Ealing and heads west to Whitland with returning milk empties in April 1955. Within the train are tanks for other destinations which will be detached en route. R.C.Riley.

Milk on the GC. Standard 4-6-0 No.73157 with a tank near Chorley Wood on 30th May 1962. Stephen Gradidge.

2800, 2917-2931, 2937-2946, 2975-2978, 2985-2994.

Siphon H 1918-20 diagram 012, running numbers:- 1422-1441.

Siphon J 1930-34 diagrams 031 and 040, running numbers:- 1215-1222, 2024-2050, 2518-2527.

Siphon G 1947-55 diagram 062 running numbers:- 1001-1051, 1310-1339, 2295-2326, 2332-2391.

By the end December 1951 the Western Region milk van fleet contained the following:

4 wheel vans - 17
6 wheel vans - 25 (from 42 at 1/1/51)
8 wheel vans - 70
8 wheel vans* - 304 (with another 20 on order)
8 wheel vans** - 30
* corridor type.
** parcel/milk vans.

LMS and BR (LMR) MILK TANKS

The original 4-wheel tanks had a capacity of 3,000 gallons; similarly the later 6-wheel vehicles. All were renumbered by the LMS in 1932/33 to bring the scattered, untidy numbering into the blocks shown below. Ex-4-wheel tanks include 44018, 44019.

44000-44069 United Dairy (70)
44075-44090 Nestles (16)
44093-44095 Nestles (3)
44097-44099 Nestles (3)
44105-44107 Nestles (3)
44150-44152 Co-operative Wholesale Society (3)
44170-44201 Express Dairy (32)
44230-44235 Express Dairy (6)
44250-44252 Cow & Gate (3)
44253-44261 United Dairy and LMSR (9)
44263-44268 railway owned (6)
44276-44285 railway owned (10)
44500-44511
44512-44561 mainly Express Dairy and United Dairy with some railway owned BR(LMR) (50)*
44562-44565

* 44512-44561 Lot 1640 built Derby 1950 had 3,000 and 2,000 gallon tank types. All had roller bearing axleboxes.

Thirteen 6-wheel wagons, similar to the tank wagon chassis, were constructed at Derby between 1935 and 1947 for the conveyance of road tankers. These were numbered 44100-44104, 44153, 44154, 44155 and 44295-44298. Ten tanks survived to become departmental/internal user vehicles during the 1980s.

Class C 31581 leaves Morden South for Kensington, in August 1959, with an empty van and a trailer tank on a flat bound eventually for somewhere on the LMR. R.C.Riley.

Upperby Black 5 No.45344 blasts through Oxenholme with empty milk tanks bound for Carlisle, on a damp July 6th 1960. Ray Farrell.

SR MILK TANKS
4401-4410; Express Dairy 4-wheel converted to six wheelers in 1938. 4409 now preserved.
4435; 6-wheel Express Dairy.
4465; 6-wheel built 1944. United Dairy.

LNER MILK TANKS
70351 6-wheel United Dairy? Cow & Gate?
70568 6-wheel Express Dairy.

BR MILK TANKS
B3138 6-wheel Unigate
B3153 6-wheel Milk Marketing Board
B3168 6-wheel Express Dairy
B3171 6-wheel built 1950 onwards. Express Dairy
B3198 6-wheel built 1950 onwards.

THE LAST DROPS
Road traffic had made for a steady erosion in milk traffic from the early 1950s and by the early '60s complacency on the part of the operating departments and rising costs generally had the Milk Marketing Board looking elsewhere for reliable transport. The costs to the dairy companies of moving the milk by rail had nearly doubled in the ten years from 1942 to 1952. Cornish milk was costing the equivalent of £1.53 per 100 gallons to transport in 1952 against an average of £0.80 in 1942. During this period the Western Region had managed *to lose* a milk train and when it eventually reached it destination the inevitable spoiling had occurred. Now this sort of perishable had once been sacrosanct and other, similar incidents, involving long delays and ineptitude did nothing to reassure the Milk Marketing Board. In BR days the daily 3.00 p.m. Cricklewood - Derby empties was diagrammed for a locomotive off Kentish Town shed, usually a Derby Class 5, but being a light train it was found to be useful for getting odd or defective locomotives back home, so releasing the diagrammed engine for something 'more useful'! Some observations during 1957 are noteworthy: 4th March - 44055 55A; 22nd May - 44676 68A; 5th June - 41195 22B; 7th June - 42951 3D; 8th June - 43048 17A; 11th June - 44467 55B; 29th July - 92131 21A. The operating side had come to regard it as a humble empty train, but these empties were vital, and needed without any delay back at the dairies. The inevitable happened when an old stager put on the job failed to make it home. This was a typically unfortunate example of the attitude of the period regarding milk trains.

In 1965 major changes were afoot, culminating in the so-called Western Agreement two years later. All milk from the West Country and west Wales was to be run over Western Region metals only, those trains formerly traversing the old LSWR main West of England line being diverted to the WR and trains running over other Regions ceasing completely.

June 1976 saw the last of the milk trains serving Vauxhall. Up until that month a milk train left Clapham Junction daily at about mid-morning for the short trip to Vauxhall where discharge could take up to three hours, after which time the empty tanks were worked into Waterloo station ready for a light engine to couple up to the rear of the train and haul it back to Clap-

On the former Great Eastern line B17 61656 LEEDS UNITED passes Westerfield Junction with milk from Halesworth for east London in May 1957. It was not unknown for this traffic to be reversed in periods of drought, when milk from the West Country would be brought into East Anglia. R.C.Riley.

61665 LEICESTER CITY with down milk empties in the rain at Bealings, on the East Suffolk line, 8th October 1956. R.C. Riley.

ham Junction. The milk receiving facilities at Vauxhall were situated beneath the viaduct and gravity was used to empty the rail tanks of their load (previously two trains had served this depot each day). At about the same time milk trains from west Wales ceased to run.

In the ten years up to 1975 the amount of milk carried by rail had fallen by nearly two-thirds, the WR having the only traffic. In October 1980

railborne milk traffic finished completely, road traffic having won the day.

Of the 170 6-wheel milk tanks surviving into 1980, 40 were chosen to be part of an MMB reserve fleet 'for emergencies'. The forty were refurbished and joined by a further 31 refurbished 4-wheel long wheelbase vehicles, oil tank chassis with re-clad milk tanks. The 'reserve fleet' was stored, awaiting use, in various parts of the West Country and some indeed saw service in

1981, transporting milk from Chard Junction to East Anglia, during a month-long dry period of the summer that year. Since then the 71 survivors have been withdrawn and sold on.

A small number of milk tanks exist today in Departmental use; those known (as at 1994) are located as follows:- W2016 - 041357 at Immingham (internal user); W2504 - 061067 at Landore; W2506 - 041358 at Hornsey; W2960 - 041348 at Immingham (internal user); W3018 - 041356 at Ferme Park; 44069 - 061007 at Old Oak Common.

Nowadays road tankers collect the milk from the farms and not one drop is transported thereafter by rail. Of course we consume less milk than we once did, gone for instance is the free school milk which accounted for a fair amount of production. Other dairy products made in more central locations do not require the intense, immediate transport of fresh milk and therefore market forces, 'structural imperatives' and all the rest mean 'on the milk' is no more.

Thanks to Roger Butcher in the preparation of this article.

Footnote
Some locations associated with the milk business are listed; it is of course by no means comprehensive but gives some indication of how

Back in London, at Queens Road, Battersea, M7 30320 with a train of milk empties ex-Vauxhall in July 1959. Adjacent to Vauxhall station was a bottling plant and pipes were run from the unloading point under the eight tracks directly into the plant. After arrival from Clapham Junction, wagons stood on the Up Windsor slow line whilst unloading and then washing out took place. Often this operation took up to four hours and when complete the train proceeded to Waterloo station where the loco ran round for the trip back to Clapham. In the 1950s two trains a day would discharge at Vauxhall, one during daylight hours and one during the early hours, each delivering 20,000 gallons or more. R.C.Riley.

B1 61187 brings a train of milk tanks round the curve at South Ruislip bound for the Independent Milk Supplies depot at Marylebone in July 1956. This train originated in Sanquhar, southern Scotland and travelled via the WCML to Bletchley thence over the Oxford line to Verney Junction. The tanks in this train had a 700 mile circuit between loadings. C.R.L.Coles.

ubiquitous the whole thing was. The scope for proper surveys of the various 'businesses' of British Railways is enormous, if extremely daunting...

Appleby, Westmorland (MR) - Express Dairy.

Ashby-de-la-Zouch, Leics (LMS-MR) - UD had milk siding.

Aspatria, Cumberland (M&C) -

Bailey Gate, Dorset (S&D) - UD had siding for tanks. Closed Jan 1969.

Basford, Cheshire - CWS had milk siding.

Bason Bridge, Wilts (S&D) - UD had siding. Milk factory opened 1909, milk tanks for London. Milk traffic ceased in October 1972.

Buckingham, Bucks - UD had a milk siding on the Banbury - Verney Jct line.

Calveley, Cheshire - UD had depot on

Up side of Crewe-Chester line 7.5 miles north of Crewe.

Carmarthen, Carm - Mutual Dairies Ltd (Unigate) had siding on Down side of SWML.

Chard Jct - Unigate had siding here until very late.

Chard Jct - UD had a tank siding here.

Congleton, Cheshire (NSR) - Nestles had siding for dairy on Up side of line.

Congleton, Cheshire (NSR) - CWS had siding for milk factory on Down side of line.

Cricklewood, London - Express Dairy had siding and Cricklewood provided a pilot for this 58070 or 58071 until Ivatt tanks 41248 or 41249 took over. Some of the milk would be tripped to Mill Hill. For many years the empties left Cricklewood every day at 3.00 p.m. for Derby.

Dolcoath, Cornwall - MMB had siding.

Dorrington, Salop (GW/LMS) - IMS had tank siding.

Ealing Broadway (West Ealing) - UD had a milk siding on Up side, east of station. Milk was off-loaded to road tankers.

Elmhurst Crossing, Staffs - milk dock on Up side of WCML.

Forest Hill, London (SR) - UD receiving dock road/rail tankers.

Frome, Somerset (GW) - ED had siding here.

Gravesend, Kent - milk receiving depot from West Country via SR.

Gillingham, Dorset (SR) - UD milk dock for road/rail tankers.

Hemyock, Devon - UD milk depot siding here (bulk supplies to Wood Lane, Vauxhall and Ilford).

Ilford, Essex - milk tank receiving depot

Lifton, Devon - milk depot. Tanks worked to Plymouth then added to Penzance- Kensington Milk.

Lostwithiel, Cornwall - Unigate milk depot siding.

Lostwithiel, Cornwall - Nestles had milk depot.

Martock, Somerset - Nestles had a milk siding.

Melksham, Wilts - CWS had milk siding.

Morden South, London - Express Dairy milk siding (tanks).

North Elmham, Norfolk - milk tank siding, milk to Ilford and London via Norwich.

Queens Park, London (LNWR) - milk off-loaded into road tankers.

Salisbury, Wilts (SR) - UD milk dock road/rail tankers.

Sanquhar, Dumfries (LMS) - IMS tank depot.

Seaton Jct, (SR) - ED milk siding for tanks.

Semley, (SR) - UD tank siding.

South Acton & Kew (LMS) - ED depot

Milk on the Midland - is this (see text) the ill-starred 3pm Cricklewood - Derby? If so, the motive power is appropriate at least - 9F 2-10-0 No.92138. Ken Fairey.

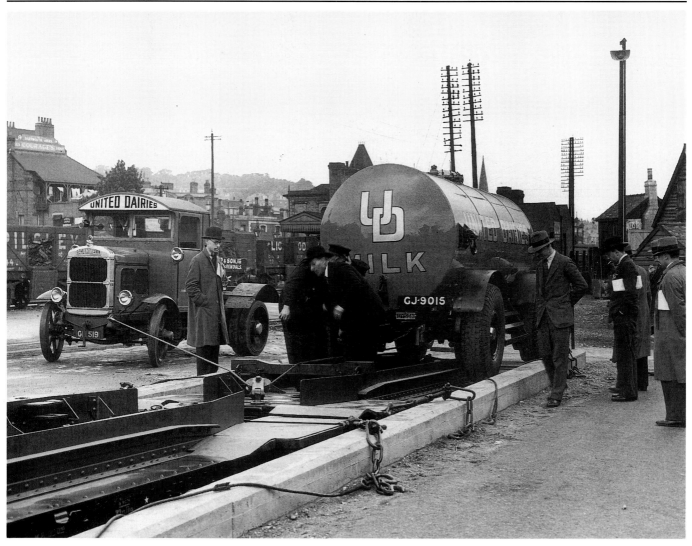

for tanks on the Richmond branch.
St Erth, Cornwall - Unigate had milk siding.
St Erth, Cornwall - United Dairies had siding.
Sturminster Newton, (S&D) - MMB had siding.
Totnes, Devon - milk depot.
Tredegar Road Bow, London - Nestles had a milk siding.
Tutbury, Staffs (NSR) - Nestles milk depot.
Wallingford, Berkshire - Co-op (CWS) had a milk siding.
West Ealing, London - milk siding.
Whitland, Carmarthenshire (GWR)- had UD depot on Up side of line east of station.
Wincanton, (S&D) - C&G had siding which opened 1933, milk tanks.
Wood Lane, London - Unigate milk receiving depot (tanks).
Wootton Bassett, Wilts - UD had tanks only milk siding.
Yetminster, Dorset (GWR) - UD had tanks only milk siding.

Abbreviations:
A&B = Aplin & Barrett Ltd.
C&G = Cow & Gate
CWS = Co-op Wholesale Society
ED = Express Dairy
IMS = Independent Milk Supplies
UD = United Dairy
UG = Unigate

Above:- The Southern may have been slow to introduce the 'fixed' milk tank but they were the first railway to provide wagons - 'Rotanks' - specifically built to transport road milk tankers. This is a demonstration staged at Forest Hill in 1933, two years after introduction, to show to the powers-that-be how the road trailers were loaded onto the rail wagons. The road tractor (notice its solid tyres) had a steel hawser to pull the trailer onto the wagon. Steel drum wheels on the trailer (just visible behind the tyres and surrounding the brakes) aligned with centrally fixed ramped rails on the wagon lifted the road wheels so that all the weight was taken off the tyres. The road trailers were designed and built by R.A.Dyson & Co. Eight adjustable shackles and chains secured the trailer tank to the rail wagon. J.Tatchell collection.

Below:- And for our friends Down-under. This is how the Australians transported their milk. The vehicle, incidentally, was built in England.

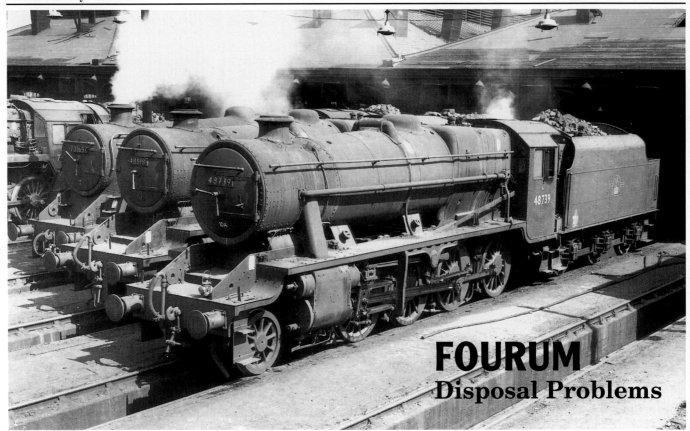

FOURUM
Disposal Problems

Above:- Willesden shed nearing the end of its days, on 31st July 1965. This was the fine sight awaiting a covert walk along the canal, the engines standing on a former extension of the shed, long cleared away - this part had once been under cover, albeit in the northlight pattern roofing style of Webb, rather than the grander style of Ramsbottom, his predecessor. The Webb type roof still survived, as seen here, in 1965, though it had not long to go - witness the leaning smokepots. Dirt and decay characterised the place at the end and with London wages and the easy availability of jobs in the 1960s staff for servicing were hard to find. It wasn't easy - much of the disposing at Willesden was undertaken by special sets of men who did nothing else. This would often cause problems in itself, as they worked on a piecework basis (i.e. an agreed number of locos constituted a shift's work) with the result that at busy times there could be serious congestion on the ashpits. It then became necessary to find a set of train men who still had an hour or so left over from their turn to 'fill in'. Photograph Peter Groom.

Below:- 45310 amid the usual yard clutter. In general many drivers objected to disposing of engines - who wouldn't, for it was a dirty and unpleasant task at the best of times and in windy weather was even worse. The late Colonel Rudgard, when Motive Power Superintendent, was very much in favour of all disposal and preparation being carried out by specialist staff - though his concerns derived mainly from the fact that it should not be done by comparatively highly paid staff who should properly be employed working trains. This was, of course, a counsel of perfection, for though such a system could be applied economically (more or less) at the major sheds it would not have been viable at smaller places - and the unions would certainly not have countenanced fish for one and fowl for another! Photograph John Wiseman.vanished ones, but whatever, Judith didn't seem worried overmuch in 1964! Photograph John Wiseman.

Above:- Ready in the yard at Willesden, with 45620 NORTH BORNEO and Stanier 2-6-0 42978. At some places a compromise was effected, which seemed to suit everyone - at Kentish Town for instance, top link men normally worked two lodge turns per week, either London - Leeds or London - Manchester and then filled in the two remaining days, normally Wednesday and Saturday with local jobs, carriage shunting at St. Pancras and ashpit duties. The double home turns were of course mileage jobs and included preparation of the engine but not disposal. Even so, one could expect to complete the turn well within 8 hours. The odd days were paid at hourly rate and any time to spare would be filled up by disposing of anything which the foreman decided wanted doing. The problem with employing special staff for disposal duties was that the workload varied so much that, in order to avoid congestion, staffing levels had to be adequate to cope with maximum demand, the result being that there would be long periods when the men would have little or nothing to do. It was a much more economical proposition to utilise a couple of enginemen who had, say a couple of hours left to complete their day! Photograph John Wiseman.

Below:- Strangely enough most drivers never raised any objections to *preparing* their own engines - indeed in my experience most of them preferred to do so, presumably on the grounds that if you want a job doing .. do it yourself! Weighty matters indeed, if long-vanished ones, but whatever, Judith didn't seem worried overmuch in 1964! Photograph John Wiseman.

Station Survey

The city with the granite heart (much of its surroundings were indeed granite, though the city itself sat on rock with an even more contorted history) could produce some appropriately stirring railway images. This is No.44980, one of Perth's vast Black Five complement, awaiting departure with the 5.30pm *Granite City* for Glasgow Buchanan Street, 29th July 1953. Photograph Brian Morrison.

ABERDEEN JOINT

by Keith G. Jones and Oswald Patterson

Aberdeen, lying between the Rivers Dee and Don, has variously been described as the 'Granite City', the 'Silver City with the Golden Sands' or, somewhat less poetically, the 'City by the Grey North Sea'. Nowadays, though, it is more likely to be referred to as Europe's North Sea oil capital - with house prices to match.

Aberdeen's early prosperity was based on sea trading links with Northern Europe - particularly the Baltic countries - and America. The city grew rapidly in the 19th century as its textile, paper, granite and fishing industries developed; it also gained considerable importance as an educational, business, administrative and agricultural centre, serving a large hinterland. Much of the growth was generated by the development of the railway network but, that said, for a city of such importance, Aberdeen did not appear on the railway map until relatively late.

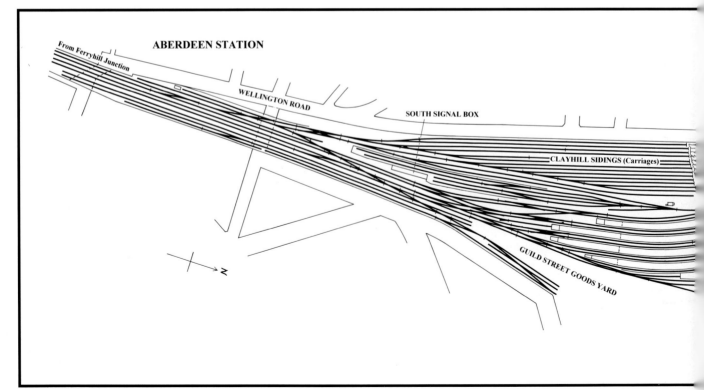

The Background

The first railway company to reach Aberdeen was the appropriately-named Aberdeen Railway, which completed its line from Guthrie (between Forfar and Arbroath) in March 1850 - the final stage in the provision of a direct rail link with London. The original terminus in Aberdeen was at Ferryhill but, following the eventual completion of work on a series of brick archways, Ferryhill was superseded in August 1854 by new premises at Guild Street, a little over half a mile to the north and at a far more central location. In 1856 the Aberdeen Railway became part of the Scottish North Eastern Railway which, in August 1865, was amalgamated with the Caledonian Railway.

The second railway company in Aberdeen was the Deeside Railway, which opened from Ferryhill to Banchory in September 1853, and extended to the new Guild Street station at Aberdeen the following year. At the Banchory end, the line was extended (by means of subsidiary companies) to Aboyne in 1859 and Ballater in 1866. Also in 1866, the Deeside Railway was leased to the Great North of Scotland Railway, full ownership ensuing in 1876.

As for the GNSR itself, its main line from Aberdeen opened as far as Huntly in September 1854 and on to Keith in October 1856. The GNSR's initial terminus in Aberdeen was at Kittybrewster, but the line was soon extended - along the bed of the abandoned Aberdeen Canal - to a new terminus at Waterloo Quay. The Waterloo extension opened to goods traffic in September 1855 and to passenger traffic in April 1856.

The two Aberdeen termini - Guild Street and Waterloo - were about half a mile apart. The only rail connection between the two was by means of the Aberdeen Harbour lines, which had been laid by the GNSR following an

Rebuilding work at the Joint station, laid bare without its roof.

agreement with the Harbour Commissioners. The connection was, however, for use only by goods traffic, passengers wishing to undertake a through journey having to make their own way between the two termini. The Aberdeen Harbour lines, incidentally, remained horse-worked until 1915, when the GNSR put into service its X (LNER Z4) class 0-4-2Ts.

The two railway companies at Aberdeen were aware of the inconvenience to passengers, which was augmented by the GNSR's renowned penchant for regarding timetables as works of fiction - the late E.L. Ahrons remarked that, in the early years, the company's stopping trains *'...could not even be dignified with the word "slow". They set the pace of a glacier, only the glacier would possibly have got there first'*. Indeed, GNSR trains arriving at Water-

loo often left passengers precious little time to sprint the half-mile to Guild Street for connections to the south.

That said, legend has it that GNSR trains *from* Waterloo invariably departed on time, and if an SNER train from the south were late arriving at Guild Street (a not-unknown occurrence!), passengers wishing to travel onwards from Waterloo were faced with a dash in the opposite direction. In such instances, GNSR staff at Waterloo weren't exactly over-helpful, as it was allegedly their custom to slam and lock the gates of the station bang on time, even if prospective passengers were to be seen struggling along the quayside towards the station.

To many, it must have seemed as if the SNER and the GNSR were striving to be obstructive, not only towards passengers, but also towards each

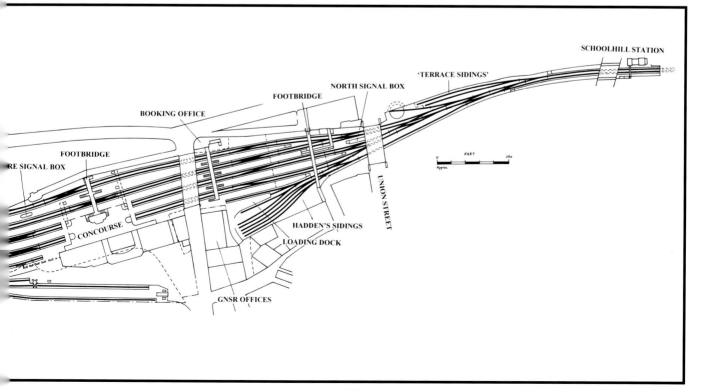

The station, north end. Date given is 1912 - note GNoSR stock in foreground. Photograph collection R.M. Casserley.

other. The two companies had, however, held regular discussions about a possible connecting line and a new joint station, though the talks had borne little fruit. The likelihood of an agreement was hardly assisted by the GNSR's refusal, until 1859, to join the Railway Clearing House. In pre-RCH days, the GNSR pooh-poohed an apportionment of the rates for through traffic, and made deliberate attempts to forward traffic to the south by sea from Aberdeen. A fine example of how not to get on with one's neighbour!

In 1861, however, the GNSR and SNER were effectively forced to put

their corporate heads together and strive for improvements at Aberdeen. In that year, the Inverness & Perth Junction Railway (later part of the Highland Railway) was incorporated to build a line between the communities of its title, and the two major companies serving Aberdeen realised that, unless considerable improvements were made in the city, the I&PJR route would abstract much of the through traffic.

To counter the threat from the I&PJR, the SNER and GNSR formulated plans for a connecting line at Aberdeen, but the latter company rejected the pro-

posed terms. The SNER, exasperated by the GNSR's awkwardness, subsequently promoted a completely new line (albeit in the name of a subsidiary company, the Scottish Northern Junction Railway) between Limpet Mill, three miles north of Stonehaven and Kintore, on the GNSR's main line north-west of Aberdeen - in other words, by-passing Aberdeen completely.

The Limpet Mill Scheme, as it was known, obtained provisional powers, but no construction was permitted for six months. If, during that period, a Bill for an alternative route through

The new station, with roof taking shape, 9th February 1914.

LNER days and 6877, one of the three D38 4-4-0s which seldom seemed long absent from Aberdeen.

through Aberdeen, starting at a junction with the SNER 22 chains south of Guild Street terminus and finishing at a junction with the GNSR, 19 chains to the north of Kittybrewster station. The new joint station was 16 chains from the junction with the SNER line. The line to the south of the station was for use by the SNER, that to the north of the station by the GNSR, but neither company was to have formal running powers over the other's tracks beyond the station area.

The GNSR subscribed the greater proportion of the funds for the line's construction - £125,000, equivalent to the cost of the aborted 'Circumbendibus' route - as opposed to the SNER's £70,000. Of the total, £83,000 was earmarked for the actual cost of the works (including the station), the other £112,000 being required for the purchase of land and property. Although part of the route passed through tunnels, any railway company wishing to bore a tunnel was under a legal obligation to purchase the whole of the properties under which the tunnel was to pass.

The first sod was cut in May 1865. The civil engineer in charge was John Willett who, earlier, had been among those unimpressed by the GNSR's proposed 'Circumbendibus' route. Willett's residence at 30 Albyn Place had been under construction at the time the 'Circumbendibus' had been proposed and, as the railway would have passed directly through the site, building had been delayed for almost two years until the controversy had ended.

The construction of the Denburn Valley line necessitated the culverting of the Denburn (a stream originating some miles to the west of Aberdeen) to the north of the station and the diversion of the southern section of the stream (in culvert) directly into the

Aberdeen was deposited, the powers for the Limpet Mill scheme were to remain in abeyance until the alternative proposal had been withdrawn or rejected. The conditional approval of the Limpet Mill scheme was, in effect, a 'stick and carrot' approach, but it had the desired effect on the GNSR.

The Missing Link

Faced with threats of competition from more than one source, the GNSR made its plans for a connecting line at Aberdeen. Earlier discussions had focused on the logical route - along the Denburn Valley - but the GNSR's new plans were for a less expensive, albeit extremely circuitous, route between Kittybrewster and the SNER, the connection with the latter being at its ticket platform just to the south of Guild Street station.

The GNSR's proposed route entailed a deep cutting around much of the city, and would have affected the developing residential areas in the west end which were occupied by Aberdeen's growing and influential business and professional community. Due to its character and length (two and three quarter miles), the proposed route was dubbed the 'Circumbendibus' and, predictably, it encountered considerable opposition, influential locals coming out strongly in favour of a direct line along the Denburn Valley.

The potential aesthetic appeal of the Circumbendibus' route was described in the Aberdeen Journal as having roads raised and diverted on all hands, and the whole thing looking like an earthwork round a besieged city'. The newspaper also pointed out that, with third class fares of 1d per mile, a journey via the 'Circumbendibus' would cost passengers a penny ha'penny

more than a direct route along the Denburn Valley.

The GNSR obtained powers for the 'Circumbendibus' - thereby quashing the Limpet Mill Scheme - but it was clear to all that the circuitous route was far from ideal. Consequently, the companies concerned bowed to public opinion and agreed instead on a connecting line through the Denburn Valley, complete with a new joint station. The new line was promoted under the name of the Denburn Valley Railway, and was incorporated on 23 June 1864.

The DVR was authorised to construct the one and three quarter mile long line

The concourse, a splendid tracery of girdering.

J36 0-6-0 No.64573 lurks at the Aberdeen bounds, 19th April 1954. Photograph John Robertson.

Upper Harbour. Of the tunnels, that at Woolmanhill was constructed by the 'cut and cover' method and, in an attempt to minimise the noise from trains passing under the Royal Infirmary, the rails were laid on longitudinal sleepers on a bed of engine ash ballast. Initially, trains passing through the tunnel were subjected to a 6mph speed limit, and engine drivers were liable to a swingeing £2 fine if they sounded their whistles in the tunnel.

As already mentioned, on 10 August 1865 - soon after the construction work had commenced - the SNER became part of the Caledonian Railway. The line, complete with the new joint station, was inspected for the Board of Trade by Lt Col Hutchinson on 22 July 1867. Unfortunately, a portion of Maberley Street tunnel had collapsed the previous day, but there were also a few other points which didn't find favour with the inspector: *'South Cabin - the points require locking with the signals...North Cabin - north distant signal requires shifting so as to render it visible from the cabin ...Kittybrewster Cabin - the points to be altered so as to prevent a goods line train from being run into by a main line train; the rods of the points in most cases require adjustment...Cast Iron Bridge at 1m 17ch - the girders are not quite up to the requisite strength; unless the company guarantee that no engine having a greater weight than 13 tons on its driving wheels shall be used on the line, some means must be adopted for strengthening (the girders)...'.* Frustratingly for latter-day researchers, Hutchinson's report made no reference to the works at the new station.

The line was reinspected on 10 September, but Lt Col Hutchinson was a mite concerned with the rebuilding of the tunnel and reserved judgement in case there was any movement in the masonry work. He returned on 29 September but all seemed satisfactory. He nevertheless required an undertaking to be furnished that a watchman would be employed at the tunnel during the winter so that, in the event of any cave-in, the drivers of approaching trains could be warned.

The New Station - 'A Very Lovely Bustling Appearance'

The new line - and the joint station - opened without ceremony on 4 November 1867. The old termini at Guild Street and Waterloo were retained, but only for use as goods stations. The new joint station was described in the *Aberdeen Journal* as being *'unsurpassed, except in size, by any other in the three Kingdoms'*, the *'proportions being such that few stations in the Kingdom will be surpassed in elegance'*. The *Journal* added that the premises *'presented a very lovely bustling appearance, and at night, when fully lighted up, the red and green lights, as displayed from Union Bridge, have quite a picturesque effect'*.

The layout of the station was unusual, for although there were three through roads, only one was provided with a platform. There were, however, two terminal bays at each end of the station. It was covered by an imposing 70ft-high arched roof, 500ft long and with an inside width of 102ft. The main station buildings were on the eastern side; their facade was constructed of dressed ashlar granite - which had been quarried at Kemnay (on Donside) - and surrounded by a balustrade of dressed freestone.

The station was administered by a Joint Committee of GNSR and Caley officials. The committee was responsible for appointing station staff, but although the signalmen at the north and south cabins were regarded as Joint Committee employees, they were appointed and paid by the respective railway companies.

Although the new station received glowing epithets from the *Aberdeen Journal*, operational problems were soon encountered. The bay platforms were too short for main line expresses, their inflexible designation ruling out any improvisation when the need arose.

Matters were not helped when, in 1878, the North British Railway started to exercise its running powers over the Caledonian (ex-SNER) line between Kinnaber Junction (near Montrose) and Aberdeen. At first, the NBR operated only goods trains through to Aberdeen, but in 1883 the company introduced a service of four daily passenger trains each way between Aberdeen and Dundee. The interests of the North British were effectively looked af-

Only six N14 0-6-2Ts were built by the North British in 1909, and three of them passed into BR stock at nationalisation in 1948. By 1953, when this photograph was taken, No.69125 was the last, and due for withdrawal any day. In quite good external condition at least, the old stager heads through Aberdeen station on 29th July 1953, hauling empty carriage stock. Photograph Brian Morrison.

A2 Pacific 60528 TUDOR MINSTREL, in blue livery, leaving Aberdeen with a relief to the 5.18pm to Edinburgh, 12th April 1954. Photograph John Robertson.

ter by the Caley, but as the NBR was not a member of the Joint Committee it had to pay tolls for the use of station facilities.

Congestion at Aberdeen Joint station increased steadily. Somewhat ironically, the situation deteriorated in the late 1880s as a direct result of the GNSR's long-overdue revision of its operations. GNSR train services had gained an abysmal reputation but, following the appointment of William

Moffatt as General Manager, the proverbial new leaf was turned. In the words of E.L.Ahrons, the company's services quickly changed from *'bad to excellent'*.

Among Moffatt's enterprising schemes were the suburban services from Aberdeen to Dyce - 'The Subbies' - introduced in 1887. They were followed in 1894 by 'Subbies' to Culter, on the Deeside line. The services were worked initially by 0-6-0Ts but, from

1893, 0-4-4Ts (later LNER 'G10' class) took over; by 1902 there were fifty-two 'Subbie trainies' in and out of the Joint station each weekday. The 'reborn' GNSR also attracted an increasing quantity of fish traffic - 6,000 tons from Aberdeen to the south in 1885 rising tenfold by 1915, plus through traffic from the Moray Firth coast and Buchan lines. All very good for the GNSR's accountants and shareholders, but very troublesome indeed for

Looking south from the station in the 1930s.

A Reid North British J35/4, 0-6-0 No.64482, heads through Aberdeen station on 20th May 1952, with southbound vans (mainly fish) from Fraserburgh. Photograph Brian Morrison.

those trying to keep things flowing at the station.

Another new traffic at the station - albeit only on a once-daily basis - was the 'Up Special Travelling Post Office'. Aberdeen became the northern terminus of the TPO in 1885, the train leaving Euston at 8.30pm and arriving in Aberdeen at 9.55am. That service was substantially accelerated over the years, and was eventually augmented by a sorting carriage attached to the 10.00pm ex-Euston. Yet another TPO vehicle ran on an evening roster from Carlisle to Aberdeen and back, while a TPO between Aberdeen and Elgin lasted only from 1886 to 1916.

The not-infrequent Royal Trains to and from Ballater, on the Deeside line, usually avoided the problems at Aberdeen by reversing at Ferryhill. Queen Victoria was therefore spared adding her voice to the debate about the congestion. This had become, particularly after the introduction of the 'Subbies', increasingly acute. As a partial solution, from September 1893 passengers could escape delays by alighting at the GNSR's new station at Schoolhill, a little to the north of the joint station and at the southern portal of Woolmanhill Tunnel. Schoolhill station was convenient for the shopping and commercial areas of Aberdeen and also served as ticket platform (a role it fulfilled until 1930 when platform barriers were installed at the joint station) and, from 1906, it was the terminus of the GNSR omnibus services.

Despite the problems at the joint station, it appears that there were very few railway accidents there during the nineteenth century. Indeed, only three incidents came to the attention of the

Board of Trade, which routinely investigated almost every mishap on Britain's railway network. One occurred a little to the south of Denburn Junction signalbox in July 1882, and another at almost the very same spot on 15 September 1883. On the latter occasion, the GNSR's 7.15pm train from Ballater collided with an empty NBR train which was being backed out of the station and across from the down to the up line on its way to the carriage sidings. Three passengers complained of being slightly shaken but, otherwise, there were no injuries. Major Marindin, who reported on the accident for the Board of Trade, opined that the collision was due to sloppy working practices, the NBR train and a home signal having been devoid of lights on a rather foggy morning. The GNSR locomotive, incidentally, was 2-4-0 No 25, its train comprising 1 brake van, 1 third-class, 1 first-class, 1 goods van, 1 third-class, 1 first-class, 1 third-class brake, 1 third-class, 1 third-class brake, 1 third-class, 2 first-class and a rear brake van - 13 vehicles in all, of which seven carriages had been added at Banchory.

Another accident occurred on 5 June 1890, the GNSR 1.00pm train from Peterhead, hauled by 4-4-0 No 5 (later LNER 'D46' class No 6805), colliding with the tail of the 12.55pm passenger train from Keith a little to the north of the joint station. Three passengers - one in the leading train and two in the Peterhead train - were slightly injured. The ensuing report explained that the Keith train had been kept standing at a distant signal, out of sight and sound of Aberdeen North cabin, for four minutes. Major Marindin's report con-

cluded that: 'The collision was due to a failure of the block working between Kittybrewster south cabin and Aberdeen North cabin, for which the only person responsible was the signalman in the former cabin, an old and experienced servant, of excellent character, who had at the time been on duty for 90 minutes, and who gave his evidence in a very straightforward manner, and did not attempt to throw blame upon any other person'. Nevertheless, the Major considered that the collision would almost certainly have been averted if the GNSR had adopted the usual practice of treating a distant signal as a warning or indicating signal, and not as an absolute stop.

Again, the formation of the two trains (as listed in the accident report) is interesting. The Peterhead train comprised 1 brake van, 1 composite carriage, 1 third-class brake carriage, 1 first-class, 1 third-class and a brake van. The Keith train consisted of 10 fish trucks, 1 composite carriage, 1 brake van, 1 third-class brake, 1 third-class, 1 first-class, 2 brake vans, 1 third-class, 1 first-class, 1 third-class brake, 1 empty brake and 1 empty horse-box - a total of 22 vehicles.

Despite the clamour for improvements to Aberdeen Joint station, the premises were in the limelight for a different reason in 1895. On the night of 22/23 July of that year, the celebrated 'races' between the West Coast companies (the LNWR and Caley) and the East Coast companies (the GNR, NER and NBR) reached their climax when the West Coast team managed a journey time of 8 hours 32 minutes for the 539-mile London - Aberdeen trip. That effectively brought an end to the racing. The time, incidentally, was not bettered by any scheduled working until the introduction of Inter-City '125s' in the 1970s!

Although the racing ended in 1895, the Caley and the NBR continued their rivalry to provide the best services between Aberdeen and the south. In 1905 the Caley introduced its 'Grampian Corridor' expresses, formed of twelve-wheeled carriages and including a restaurant car. The NBR's answer were the fixed-formation 'Aberdeen Block Trains', made up of the largest and most comfortable stock yet owned by the company. In 1906, the NBR introduced its impressively-proportioned (but initially disappointing) Atlantics, one of their intended duties being the Aberdeen - Edinburgh run.

Major Rebuilding

After much public and press criticism of the station during the 1890s, the railway companies entered into extensive discussions and, in 1899, powers were obtained for a major upgrading of the city's railway facilities. Among the authorised improvements were the widening of the approach lines from Ferryhill Junction, and the provision of additional siding accommodation at the south end of the station, the latter work requiring the closure or diversion of several roads.

One point which caused concern was the arrangement for loading fish on to trains at the station: *'Apart from the objections to this being carried on within the station buildings proper, there is the question of danger to passengers going to and from the station. The haste, in many cases amounting to recklessness, with which the fish lorries are driven along the approach to the station while numbers of passengers are going to or coming from trains is undoubtedly a menace to public safety'.*

The solution to that problem was the provision of special fish loading docks, located so as to obviate congestion in Market Street and Guild Street. To further ensure that the buildings of the proposed new station would be retained purely for passenger traffic, the GNSR eventually laid new loading docks and carriage storage sidings at the site of the former Hadden Mills, to the north-east of the station.

Work on improving the southern approaches to the station commenced in 1902. At the Ferryhill end a viaduct with granite arches replaced the old brick-arched viaduct, the new structure accommodating four main lines and a siding instead of two lines and a siding. By 1904 work was in hand to widen Guild Street bridge, above the joint station.

The GNSR was also active in the hotel market, purchasing the Station Hotel in Guild Street in 1910. The company had, in 1890, acquired the prestigious Palace Hotel in Union Street; it had reopened in 1891 and had subsequently been connected to the station by a covered walkway which gave patrons direct access to and from trains.

The final plans for the 'new' station were not published until 1911, although some improvements had already been made. In July 1908 new platforms had been opened (on the west side of the station) for suburban traffic while, a year later, new suburban station buildings - built of 'white' Kemnay granite - had been completed. Initially, the new buildings had been connected by footbridge only to the suburban platforms (latterly Nos 7 and 8 for Dyce trains and No 9 for Deeside services), but the footbridge was later extended to the main concourse. The new buildings fell into disuse after the cessation of suburban services in 1937, but they still survive today, albeit as a hairdressers' salon.

The rebuilding of the station was virtually complete by May 1915, and the works were duly inspected by Lt Col Druitt for the Board of Trade: 'There are two pairs of lines through the station, viz: the West main lines and the Main lines, each pair being provided with scissors crossings. With the exception of the down West Main line, which is signalled in one direction only, all these through lines are signalled both for arrival and departure. The down west passenger platform is 850 feet long, the island platform between the up west main line and the down main line is 1400 feet long, and the platform adjoining the up main line is 1585 feet long [also quoted as 1596ft - and still one of the longest in Britain today]. At the south end of the station there are also 5 passenger bay lines, signalled for both arrival and departure, the adjoining platforms varying from 620 to 720 feet in length.

'The main approach to the station is from Guild Street, on the east

B12 No.61502 ready to depart Aberdeen on 29th July 1953 with the 6.10pm train to Keith. Photograph Brian Morrison.

A2 Pacific No.60531 BAHRAM waits to leave Aberdeen with the 7.10pm *Aberdonian* for London, 30th July 1953. Photograph Brian Morrison.

side...there is a semi-circular booking hall, good waiting rooms with conveniences of both sexes, bath rooms, lavatories etc. There is also a booking office on the west side of the station, approached from Bridge Street.

'There is a large central concourse between the booking office and up main line platform, and the various platforms are approached by means of a foot overbridge, with flights of stairs to each platform, opposite the booking office on the west side. There is also a foot bridge leading from the main platform on the east side, with flights of stairs leading to the main island platform and the down west passenger line platform.

'There are three signal-boxes for working the traffic at the station, viz:-

(1) Denburn South Junction, which controls all the traffic in and out of the station at the South end; this is a new box, containing 217 working levers, 19 spare levers, and 4 spaces. [The 'box - later known as Aberdeen South - had opened on 31 May 1914 and had become fully operational on 28 June. It was replaced by a new LMSR-style structure on 20 April 1947].

(2) Aberdeen Central Box, which works the scissors crossings between each pair of through lines and the signals connected therewith, and also slots all the incoming signals for the through lines. This box contains 60 levers, all in use. [It had been brought

into use on 4 October 1914, replacing two older 'boxes - Aberdeen Station and Aberdeen West.]

(3) Aberdeen North Box, which works the traffic at the north end of the station, both in and out; it is provided with a new frame containing 127 levers in use and 23 spare. [operational 24 August 1914].

'There are also two ground frames of 4 levers each, for working the scissors crossings at the end of the South bay lines; these frames are electrically controlled from the Denburn South Junction Box'.

Lt Col Druitt noted that the signalman's view of trains standing in the five bay lines at the south end of the station was very restricted, and recommended that track circuiting be installed for all five roads. Apart from that, he was quite satisfied.

The thirteen platforms had a total length of over two miles, and a combined surface area of some four acres. The platform designations were:
Nos 1 to 5 - south facing bays for NBR, Caley and Deeside services
Nos 6 to 8 - through platforms (No 6 was the main arrival platform for north AND south trains)
No 9 - shorter through platform
Nos 10 to 13 - north facing bays for GNSR trains.
As previously indicated, platforms 7, 8 and 9 were principally allocated to suburban services. From the con-

course, the platforms extending north and south were protected by umbrella roofs for almost their entire lengths.

Ironically, because of the reduction in railway services during the Great War, the new station wasn't over-used at first. During the war, however, no less than 185 ambulance trains arrived at Aberdeen, conveying 21,627 sick or wounded soldiers.

A New Regime
At the grouping, the station became joint LMSR/LNER property. Before too long, the competition offered by motor bus operators (in which the railway companies themselves were major shareholders) resulted in a gradual decline in the patronage of the 'Subby' services, and these were withdrawn in April 1937. Subsequently, platforms 7, 8 and 9 at the Joint station saw little passenger use. During their last years, the 'Subbies' had been serviced by a motley collection of rolling stock of mixed GNSR and GER origin - a less attractive proposition to the travelling public than modern double-deck buses.

Another traffic loss of the period concerned fish. In 1937 the road haulier, Charles Alexander, obtained licences to convey Aberdeen fish to Manchester and elsewhere in North-west England, and other local hauliers soon followed his lead. Although the railway companies retained most of the London fish traffic, overall revenues were much reduced.

In contrast, the main line services to and from Aberdeen thrived. They benefited from modern locomotives and rolling stock, among the engines being Gresley's part-streamlined 'P2' 2-8-2s. The 'P2s' were, however, not particularly successful on the Edinburgh - Aberdeen section, and were later rebuilt by Edward Thompson as 4-6-2s. More successful were Gresley's much under-rated 'V2' 2-6-2s, which were first allocated to Aberdeen in 1937 and went on to perform sterling work on the main line almost until the end of the steam era. On services by the LMSR route, ex-Caley 4-4-0s and 4-6-0s were gradually displaced by Compound 4-4-0s, Crab 2-6-0s and, later, Black Fives and Jubilees with intermittent visits by Royal Scots and Pacifics.

During World War II the station eluded the best efforts of the Luftwaffe, although in 1941 the LNER's Palace Hotel was destroyed by fire. Despite remaining virtually unscathed, the station nevertheless featured in a post-war scheme for the extensive rebuilding of central Aberdeen. The grand plan included the relocation of the existing terminal building to the north side of Guild Street, the town planning consultants, Messrs Chapman and Riley, considering that the rail-borne visitor... 'having been first confronted by a queue of fish lorries...can reach Union Street only by a tiresome uphill walk as an alternative to a trifling bus ride'.

It was proposed to rebuild the station on three levels. The lower level was to comprise the main station and yard, vehicular approach, booking hall and other facilities and platforms. The intermediate level was to contain the concourse, a restaurant, and a large car park area above the platforms. The top level was to include escalator access from Union Street, at either side of the new Palace Hotel (which would replace the original hotel). It was also planned to build a bus station in the existing station yard (one was provided, but not until 1963) and to provide a fish handling area, with harbour facilities, in the Torry area, to be served by a branch line along the south bank of the River Dee from Craiginches.

Somewhat fortunately, the grandiose scheme failed to come to fruition. Given the widespread move to road transport as the 1950s progressed, the massive cost of the works would, with the benefit of hindsight, have surely become the subject of severe scrutiny.

The BR Years

The all-too-familiar story of run-down branch and secondary lines affected the north-east of Scotland as much as it affected other parts of Britain. Despite a modest increase in railway use after the introduction of diesel services in the late 1950s, the traffic at Aberdeen Joint station showed an overall drop during the decade. Nevertheless, the station was a very interesting place for observers during the 1950s and 1960s.

In early BR days, the majority of GNS Section services were still in the hands of veteran D40 and D41 class 4-4-0s or B12 4-6-0s, the B12s having been transferred from the GE Section in the 1930s and 1940s. Thompson B1s had made their debut on the GNS Section in 1946 but, by 1948, there were still not enough of them to replace the older 4-4-0s and 4-6-0s.

The B1s were not the only new arrivals at Aberdeen in the early BR era. Nine K2 2-6-0s were transferred to the GNS Section from 1952 onwards, some allocated to Kittybrewster shed but others to Keith. In 1953 eight ex-NBR Glen (D34) 4-4-0s were transferred to Kittybrewster to supplement the B1s; they were used on local passenger and freight duties and, during the late 1950s, pilot duties at the north end of the joint station. Other 4-4-0s - this time ex-LMSR 2Ps - were also drafted to the area in the early 1950s, and saw considerable service, on the Buchan lines in particular. Later in the 1950s, 4MT 2-6-4Ts and 2-6-0s were drafted to Kittybrewster shed.

The passenger workings to and from the south end of the joint station were of an entirely different character. Until 1958 the Aberdeen - Edinburgh trains routinely changed engines at Dundee and, consequently, Ferryhill or Tay Bridge A2s and V2s monopolised the workings. From 1958 Haymarket Pacifics worked through to Aberdeen far more regularly but, as we shall see later, engines from farther afield also appeared at Aberdeen with reasonable regularity.

By the late 1950s the Aberdeen - Glasgow services were usually entrusted to Standard or ex-LMSR Class 5 4-6-0s, the Standards including the ten Scottish-based examples fitted with Caprotti valve gear, Nos 73145-54. By then, Coronation Pacifics and Jubilees

The middle 1950s, and buses above the North box.

J39 0-6-0 No.64975 of Ferryhill heads a southbound mixed freight through the station on 20th May 1952. Photograph Brian Morrison.

had seen their domination of the 'Postal' fall to the 5MTs, then Gresley V2s. However, sightings of Pacifics, Jubilees and also Royal Scots in Aberdeen could still be almost guaranteed on Glasgow Fair Saturdays during the latter half of the 1950s, when some twenty specials brought Glaswegians to the Granite City for a dose of North Sea ozone.

The station area at Aberdeen was always busy with shunting and empty stock movements. At the south end, much of the work was undertaken by ex-NBR N15 0-6-2Ts or Ferryhill's two J39s, Nos 64795 and 64975. The shunting and pilot activities at the north end of the station were more varied, and were sometimes entrusted to engines running in after a visit to Inverurie Works. The adjacent Guild Street yard was normally worked by ex-Caley 0-6-0Ts, while trip working from Craiginches to Kittybrewster was usually performed by Ferryhill- or Kittybrewster based J35s, J36s, or WD 2-8-0s. These trains used the through tracks alongside Platforms 8 and 9.

The Day to Day

Noteworthy comings and goings at Aberdeen were, like anywhere else in Britain, duly reported in the railway press. The most detailed accounts were, probably, contained in the Railway Observer or Trains Illustrated, and these have been trawled for a flavour of the day to day at Aberdeen. 1952 for instance was marked by 'the commencement of a regular ex-LNER locomotive working over the ex-LMSR Aberdeen - Perth main line', involving

the 6.25am up Bon Accord and the 11.38am ex-Perth Granite City or 10.35am goods; V2 2-6-2 No.60970 of Ferryhill began the roster, but was replaced early in January by other Ferryhill 2-6-2s. Camden Pacific 46237 CITY OF BRISTOL turned up at Aberdeen on the up West Coast Postal on 18th March 1952 while on the same day the use of a B1, 61307 on the early morning train to Ballater, instead of the customary B12, was noteworthy. Kingmoor Clan Pacifics had been working into the city, and on 26 May and 12 June 1952 72009 CLAN STEWART and 72005 CLAN MACGREGOR respectively brought in the Saint Mungo from Glasgow; on 21 May the latter brought in the down Postal and left with the 9.35am Saint Mungo. 'An extra' to Kings Cross on 11th July was double-headed by '5MT No.45367 and V2 No.60931, and the 7.35pm by Compound No.41176 and V2 No.60888'. On 5 August a southbound goods from Aberdeen was headed by Eastfield 4MT No.43138 - it had arrived with a goods from Dundee, the first of its type to be seen in the Granite City. 'Spotlessly-clean' A2 No.60532 BLUE PETER worked the Royal Train from Aberdeen to Edinburgh on 12 September - this was Aberdeen's Aberdonian engine, so Haymarket's No.60537 BATCHELOR'S BUTTON 'had to be borrowed for that job from 11-14 September'; on 9 and 10 September the train was V2-hauled, piloted out of Aberdeen by 4-4-0 No.41176 and 4-6-0 No.45245 respectively...

A notable visitor at the end of November 1953 was N2 0-6-2T No.69500, passing through on its way

to Inverurie for repair. Polmadie Clan No.72000 CLAN BUCHANAN worked into Aberdeen with the Granite City on 25 December. Various new Standards were finding their way to Aberdeen and another 'first', 4MT 2-6-0 No.76000, from Motherwell, worked in with a coal train from Kelty on 6 February 1954; this was usually a WD 2-8-0 turn. A shortage of motive power at Perth resulted in the first appearance in Aberdeen, since June 1953, of a Royal Scot, 46105 CAMERON HIGHLANDER, which took out the Saint Mungo on 3 March 1954.

The observations in 1955 included the withdrawal of G5 0-4-4T No.67327 in February, after which pilot duties at the north end of Aberdeen Joint were performed by V4 No.61701, an F5, C16, J38 and even a B1. Crewe Jubilee No.45726 VINDICTIVE arrived in Aberdeen on 13 April with the 7.15am from Glasgow (Buchanan Street). On 21 June 1955 Eastfield WD 2-8-0 No.90489 worked the 8.45am Aberdeen - Banchory goods in place of the usual Glen or 2P 4-4-0 and on 27 July 1955, 71000 DUKE OF GLOUCESTER, no less, arrived with a special from Glasgow Buchanan Street, setting out for Perth in the afternoon with empty stock. It reappeared at Aberdeen on the three-coach 4.35pm local from Perth on 6 July and returned with the 9pm goods - a load of six vans and a brake!

The day to day of 1956 saw similar fare - in March, D11 No.62687 LORD JAMES OF DOUGLAS was an unusual type on station pilot work at the north end, running in after repair at Inverurie; Edge Hill Princess No.46211

QUEEN MAUD was seen at Aberdeen on 30 March 1956 with the 3.21pm from Perth, deputising for a Polmadie Clan, and Newton Heath Jubilee No.45642 BOSCAWEN arrived on 1 April with the 5.55pm from Dumfries, leaving with the return train at 10.10pm. On 29 July 1956 a Britannia, No.70052 FIRTH OF TAY headed the 5.25pm Aberdeen - Glasgow and a Haymarket A4, 60012 COMMONWEALTH OF AUSTRALIA worked into Aberdeen on 26 November, only the second time such an engine had been reported since the summer of 1954; it brought in the 10am from Edinburgh and returned south with the 3.40pm from Aberdeen.

1957 saw report of a Motherwell WD 2-10-0, No.90760, which brought a special freight from Perth into Aberdeen on 24 November, returning with another goods at 9.15pm, 'the first of its type to be seen in the Granite City for two or three years'. In March, a number of Motherwell 2-10-0s were observed on coal trains from Thornton to Craiginches down yard. In mid-May, ex-Caley 4-4-0 No.54491 was running in after repair at Inverurie on the 8.45am Aberdeen - Banchory goods. With the summer timetable, V2s became the daily motive power on the up *Postal* from Aberdeen. On 20 June 3MT 2-6-0 No.77016 became the first of its type to visit Aberdeen (it is believed to have been on its way to Inverurie for repair) and on 6 July 1957 Polmadie 4-6-2 46230 DUCHESS OF BUCCLEUCH worked the 4.45pm (SO) fish from Aberdeen as far as Perth. 'Most notable visitor' was without doubt Willesden Patriot No.45517,

early on 1 October with the previous night's fast freight from Dumfries. It returned to Polmadie with the balancing train at 10.10pm. On 7 October, A1s 60129 GUY MANNERING of Gateshead and 60160 AULD REEKIE of Haymarket reached Aberdeen; 'these days', the report ran, 'A1s rarely penetrate beyond Dundee or Perth'. On 14 November 1957 the first Stanier 2-8-0 seen at Aberdeen for some years, No.48472 of Kingmoor (then 68A in the Scottish Region) brought in a goods from Perth and left with the next day's 10.55pm Stirling goods.

During 1958 Clan Pacifics recently transferred to Haymarket shed were seen to be penetrating to Aberdeen, 72006 CLAN MACKENZIE appearing to have the regular job of the Aberdeen section of the *Night Scotsman*. On 9 February 1958, 'no fewer than six of Haymarket's Pacifics, including A4 No 60024', visited Aberdeen, normal working arrangements being badly affected by severe snowstorms. On 30 July 1958, Brush Type 2 No.D5511 was noted at Aberdeen - it was on loan to the Scottish Region for trials, and performed several duties from Aberdeen in August. In September, 'through engine working between Edinburgh (Waverley) and Aberdeen was reintroduced on a large scale for the first time since the war'. In October, English Electric Type 1 No.D8006 of Devons Road (on loan to the ScR) was tested on GNS territory, including the Fraserburgh and Deeside lines from Aberdeen. Also on loan was Type 2 No.D5303, in charge of the down *Granite City* and the 6.5pm back from Aberdeen on 26 November 1958. One

interesting event of the year, which seems to have escaped the attention of correspondents was the debut, in April, of the unique battery railcar set, SC79998/79999 on Deeside line services. The necessary battery charging equipment was installed at Platform 1 at the Joint station. The railcar set remained in use only until 1962, but was subsequently acquired for preservation and now resides at the East Lancashire Railway.

In 1959, the reports included further tastes of things to come: 'In the second week of March, new Metro-Cammell diesel twin-units began work on the Aberdeen - Ballater branch. Diesel working of the Type 2 (BR&CW) diesels on the Edinburgh - Aberdeen passenger trains began on 31/8/59...'. But it was not all doom and gloom for steam enthusiasts. Probably without doubt the most interesting regular steam workings to and from Aberdeen during the early and mid-1960s were those of the A4 Pacifics on the three-hour expresses to Glasgow (Buchanan Street). The last recorded appearances of a BR-owned A4 on the Aberdeen - Glasgow run seem to be those of No 60024 KINGFISHER on 13 and 14 September 1966 although, on 25 March 1967 the then-preserved No 60009 UNION OF SOUTH AFRICA worked a Perth - Aberdeen special. That was something of a late flourish as, in the summer of 1967, steam traction was completely eliminated from north-east Scotland.

After the wielding of the infamous Beeching axe, all secondary lines in north-east Scotland were closed by 1968. The old Caley main line between

North end layout, from Union Street bridge, 1937.

Kinnaber Junction and Stanley Junction was also dispensed with, leaving Aberdeen with services only to and from Glasgow, Edinburgh and London (all via Dundee) and Inverness.

The north bay platforms and the Haddens sidings, largely disused since the Beeching closures, were lifted in 1971, the site of the platforms later being sold for redevelopment. The track layout was further altered by the placing of a buffer stop at the north end of Platform 7, thus creating a siding. Platforms 6, 8 and 9 remained through roads, albeit leading to a single track northwards towards Dyce. In early 1973, the canopies and the footbridge connections to the former west lines booking office were demolished.

In 1981 the entire station area was resignalled and rationalised. The old signalboxes at Aberdeen South, North and Central, plus Ferryhill Junction were closed, with matters subsequently controlled from a new box brought into use on 21 June. Platforms 1 and 2 were connected to the freight lines and no longer became available for passenger trains - only mail, parcels and empty stock storage. Platform 7 was reinstated as a through line, but the tracks at Platforms 8 and 9 were lifted. Part of the track bed was given over to a head-shunt for trains entering the maintenance depot and a new carriage wash facility at Clayhills.

Aberdeen station is still known locally as the 'Joint Station'. It remains busy today, albeit with a limited variety of motive power and rolling stock. Most services are worked by Class 158 die-

V4 Mogul (one-time pilot - see text, The Day to Day) leaving Aberdeen on 26th June 1957, with the 6.25am pick-up freight for Laurencekirk. Photograph Brian Morrison.

sel units, although HST 125s are used on InterCity services to the south. The surviving sleeper service is worked by double-headed Class 37s. Perhaps ironically, the term 'Joint Station' has now acquired a new relevance. As a result of recent reorganisations in preparation for privatisation, the station is owned by Railtrack but the services are provided by ScotRail, InterCity East Coast and InterCity Cross Country...

This article is based on *The Joint Station* by Keith G.Jones, published by the GNSR Association in 1992. Additional information was culled from *History of*

the Great North of Scotland Railway by Sir Malcolm Barclay-Harvey (Locomotive Publishing Co, 1949) and *The Great North of Scotland Railway* by H.A.Vallance (David St.John Thomas, 1989). Some of the signalling information was supplied by Mr Bryan Wilson, while the Board of Trade inspection and accident reports were sourced at the Public Record Office, Kew.

Further information about the GNSR Association - one of Britain's most friendly railway associations - can be obtained from the Membership Secretary, Craighall Cottage, Guildtown, Perth PH2 6DF.

An unequivocally wonderful picture - Black Fives Nos.44957 and 44669 coming out of Aberdeen with the Saint Mungo. Photograph Brian Morrison.